Voices Re-sounding

Voices Re-Sounding

Voices Re-Sounding

Creative Monologues on Biblical Females

Bonni-Belle Pickard

VOICES RE-SOUNDING
Creative Monologues on Biblical Females

Cover painting by Lucy D'Souza-Krone. Used with permission.

ISBN: 9798342979313

Dedicated with gratitude to:

> Rev Bill Fisackerly, III,
>> who taught me to listen to the voices of scripture;
>
> Rev Mark Garrison,
>> who challenged me to articulate what I heard;
>
> Dr Carol Newsom,
>> who taught me even deeper listening
>> to the female voices of scripture.

ACKNOWLEDGMENTS

This collection of monologues has come to me over a period that spanned some 30 years, three continents, and many congregations and audiences. From the Kodaikanal International School Chapel in South India to Candler Women at Emory University and Briarcliff United Methodist Church in Atlanta; from the British Methodist Circuits of Asbury (Birmingham), Enfield and Kingston Upon Thames (London), and North Kent to the Women Ministers' Annual Gathering: my grateful thanks to all who have listened intently with me to the Voices Re-Sounding and encouraged me to keep listening.

My special thanks to Lucy D'Souza-Krone whose artwork adorns the cover. The cover illustration is part of a larger work entitled 'Women Praise God' that Lucy painted for the Diocese of Limburg, Germany in 2014. Based on Psalm 148 in which all creation praises God, Lucy particularly wanted to depict the praise of women. She includes seven women in the 'lap' of the woman at the bottom of the painting; these are meant to signify the generations of women who "praise God with their lives and everything they have" – surely including their voices! It is an important metaphor for this collection which celebrates the voices of our Biblical foremothers.

My thanks as well to Pat Oakley for her careful proofreading of this volume.

CONTENTS

INTRODUCTION

The first of the voices that came to me begging to be heard was that of Bath-Shebah. I was in South India, sitting on a well-worn pew of the Margaret Eddy Chapel at Kodaikanal International School Chapel one Sunday morning. My husband and I had worked as music teachers at the school for many years, and the wooden pews and the cool stone walls of the chapel were the backdrop of the Sunday routine that we shared with our children, co-workers, students, and friends. I often played the piano or the organ for the worship services, and my husband directed the choir; I also taught Sunday School and was on the Church Council. Several times before in the Chapel, I had felt God speaking to me in particular ways. On this Sunday morning, it was a female voice urging me to consider the scripture stories in a different way.

On this particular Sunday, we had a guest preacher who had taken the story of David and Bath-Shebah for his sermon topic. He apparently didn't know that one of our regular ministers had preached on the same lectionary reading the previous week, but I found myself increasingly agitated at hearing King David being extolled for the magnanimity in repenting of his guilt while Bath-Shebah's story of rape was seemingly dismissed as an inconvenient detail. That morning's dismissal seemed the equivalent of raping her all over again. I left the service seething with quiet anger. Bath-Shebah's voice was not to be ignored.

1

That was in the early 1990s. Some fifteen years earlier, as a teenager back in Florida, I had preached a sermon for the Youth Service at the church where my father was the minister. Though I don't remember what I preached, the sermon and the service were warmly received by the congregation. The next day, though, my high school Math teacher (who didn't attend our church), called me up to the front of the class to chastise me for preaching: didn't I know that the Bible said women were not to speak in church? I stumbled back to my seat as the room began to spin around me. No, I didn't know that. I'd never heard that from 16 years of my father's sermons. I decided to find out for myself if it were true, and if so, why that was in the Bible.

That was in the mid-1970s when feminism and Christian Feminist theology were just becoming popular. I began to immerse myself in finding out for myself what the Bible REALLY said about women. I read voraciously and went to rallies and eventually took correspondence courses in New Testament Greek and Hebrew so I could do Bible translation for myself. During that time, I also married and moved to India (where my husband had grown up as the son of missionary parents), and we had collected our children: three from my womb and three from my heart, that is, three biological offspring and three fostered/adopted. In the process, I found myself listening more carefully for the female voice in scripture.

On that Sunday in Kodai Chapel, a female voice, that of Bath-Shebah's, called out to me across the millennia. A monologue began to write itself in my head and then on paper over the next few hours. The next morning, I went to see Mark Garrison, our senior pastor, and told him what I was experiencing. He listened carefully and then invited me to give a sermon – on David and Bath-Shebah – the next Sunday. I hadn't quite expected that, but Bath-Shebah's voice was insistent on being heard.

After the service, there were many positive responses, but I remember two in particular. An Indian man with tears in his eyes told me he'd never heard a sermon that exposed the victim's side. He begged me to keep on searching out and proclaiming that perspective. The principal of the school, a thoughtful man whom I admired greatly, called me into his office the next day to thank me for the monologue. He said it was the first time he had ever heard a woman's menstrual period mentioned in church, and he wondered why it had taken so long to speak about such.

Sometime later, the second of the monologues emerged, the story of John the Baptist as 'witnessed' by a fictional woman. I had realised that presenting a female perspective was important and that I really didn't feel comfortable pretending that I was male, so just telling the story from John's perspective was not going to work. That monologue was also first presented at the Kodai School Chapel. I gathered up one of the sweeper-women's rustic brooms and literally swept my way through that monologue. Some years later, a friend (again male) sent me a letter from Phoenix, Arizona, saying he often recalled that monologue and how it made him consider his own 'beaten path.'

Discovering those biblical women's voices encouraged me to find my own voice as well. In 1998, we moved from India to Atlanta, Georgia, where I began my MDiv studies at Candler School of Theology in preparation to become a Methodist minister. Along with full-time studies, I was employed at the Briarcliff United Methodist Church as the organist, children's choir director, and a women's group leader. For my preaching classes at Candler, I also needed opportunities to practice delivering sermons, and I convinced the senior pastor to let me do a series of monologues for the Wednesday night services during Advent. By then, I knew there were four women named in Matthew's genealogy of Jesus, which coincided well with the four weeks of Advent. When I realised one of those women was Bath-Shebah, I leaned in hard to listen to the voices of Tamar and Rahab and Ruth as well. I performed each of those Advent Adventure monologues with a simple costume and a prop: a red rope for Rahab, a signet staff for Tamar, a sheaf of wheat for Ruth, each of which I quietly laid in a 'manger' at the end of the monologue. Those gathered then sang a verse of 'O Come, O Come, Emmanuel' and left in silence.

The next year I was encouraged to do another series of Advent monologues, so I chose women from Luke's Nativity story: Elizabeth, Mary, and Anna, as well as the John the Baptist from before. One woman whispered to me afterwards, "You've got to get these published!"

Other monologues began to come my way as well. I encountered Rizpah's story while reading an assignment for an Old Testament class. Each night we had about one hundred pages of scripture to speed-read, but that night, I stopped short when I spotted Rizpah's story, determined to ask my professor for more information at the next morning's class. To my horror, he skipped right over the story and proceeded to the next chapter! That afternoon, I went to the registrar's office and changed my OT class to the one taught by Carol Newsome, who had a reputation for concentrating on the *stories* in the text. The Rizpah monologue presented itself to me soon after that. That monologue format was a little different in that I found myself speaking *to* Rizpah rather than imagining what her words would be.

All of that was nearly a quarter century ago. Since then, I've moved to England where I've been a Methodist minister, and new Biblical female voices have presented themselves, which I have in turn shared with my congregations. Going through old sermon files recently, I was amazed to find nearly two dozen such monologues had emerged. During the COVID pandemic, I recorded the original Advent Adventure monologues as a series for the North Kent Methodist Circuit online services. I'm currently preparing to present that series for the Women Ministers' Annual Gathering. Each time I share them, I hear something new from these voices of the past, and I learn something new about myself and my own voice. I also realise that in the intense 'busy-ness' of being a full-time minister, when a new sermon is expected every Sunday, and Sunday comes every week, there is sadly less time to listen carefully to the voices in the stories. I'm looking forward to retiring in a few years and having more time to listen.

In the meantime, I offer you the voices of these women as I have heard them. Perhaps they will speak to you as well. And perhaps you too will find the voice God has given you to tell what God has done and is doing all around us.

==

Note: As monologues, these creations are meant to be spoken aloud, as the poetry within them only becomes fully apparent when they are heard. The words appear on the page in poetic form, which gives some clues as to how they should be spoken. If a silent reading is necessary, then a slow reading gives the greatest chance of the reader 'hearing' what is being said.

HAGAR
(Genesis 16, 21:8-21)

Hagar the Hag, they call me:
       The Old Woman, dried up and useless.
What they see
       and what God sees
       are often very different things.
They see the outside:
       skin toasted dark from the sun,
       back bent under the burdens of slavery,
       face wrinkled from the worries of life
           and motherhood and survival,
       from trials and tribulations:
But God sees the inside.
       God knows a 'hag' is a Holy One
For that is what 'Hag' means:
       one who knows the reverence of God
       as a constancy within,
       a brooding presence all around:
A Hag knows holiness.

It was not always so with me.
In my early years I was rebellious enough;
       little room for rebellion in a slave girl, though.
I went early to serve in Pharaoh's court.

He was pleased enough with me;
> he had me groomed for greater duties.

And then Master Abram came to visit —
> Master Abram was a rich man even then,

The Pharaoh was impressed with this visitor from far away,
> even if the visitor had come
>> requesting food and accommodation.

Master Abram brought Sarai Madam with him —
> such a beauty in those day!

Pharaoh took her in immediately
> and would have had her for his own
> if the Lord had not intervened in a dream:

God told Pharaoh that Sarai was really Abram's wife!

Whew! There was a storm brewing in Pharaoh's chambers then,
> but before anyone quite knew what was happening,

Pharaoh had shipped off Master Abram
> and Sarai Madam
> and all their flocks and supplies and servants –
> with me among them!

And so I came to live in Master Abram's Promised Land,
> as a slave to Sarai Madam,

Far away from my home, my people, my gods
> far away...

Sarai Madam was kind enough to me in the early days.
> Actually, I was her favourite!

Sometimes it was almost like I was her friend
> or her daughter, as she had none of the own...

We would sit, and she would talk and dream,
> and I would listen and dream my own dreams.

Sarai Madam was always busy with the household:
> training the servants, watching over the accounts
> and the cooking, the cleaning,
> the entertaining of the guests.

She had so much, and yet all she really wanted was a child,
      someone to truly call her own.
No one could blame her for that –
      for wanting a child of her own —
But that is how things changed between us.
      I, who belonged to her by law,
      would be the one to bear her a child.
'Her' child, it would be:
Hers and Abram's,
      to fulfill their longing,
      to fulfill a promise,
      to fulfill an emptiness.

And so Master Abram lay with me:
      the Venerable Old Master
      laying with me, a slave girl,
No one asked me, of course.
      A slave girl may be beautiful and fertile,
      but she has no voice.
At least no voice to question a Master
      or a Madam:
A slave is to obey,
      not to question.
The Pharaoh and my Master and my Madam all taught me
      that a slave girl may not raise her voice
         against her masters.

A slave girl may not have a voice,
      but her ears may not be so easily stopped,
And so I would hear much,
      much that would make me question.
But I would also hear my Master Abram speak of his God
      who he said would speak to him...
And I would wonder:
      Would a God who speaks also listen,
      even to a slave girl?

I was soon to find out!

My body obeyed my master's wishes,
          and soon my belly was swelling...
Sarai's wish became her woe:
The seed growing within me
          pushed us further and further apart,
          until the house was not big enough for both of us.

Sarai Madam harassed me then,
          treated me like a wild animal,
And Abram did not protest.
I endured what I could,
          but then I had to leave:
          it was more than I could bear.

I ran to the desert,
          running blindly toward the sands of Egypt.
Fierce sun above.
Feet running, running, across the burning sand,
          through the sheer vastness of it all.
Running, running
          until I found the spring.
          Until I stopped for breath,
          and for water
          and for cool.

It was there that the angel found me that first time,
There by the pool,
          the pool to which I gave a special name:
          Beer-lahai-roi,
          The Pool of the Living One who Sees Me.

For indeed, God saw me there
          and spoke to me –
          to me! A slave girl!
God spoke to me,
          quietly, assuredly,
And God blessed me
          and promised me that my son would be blessed...

And then sent me back.

It was strange to go back,
       but a slave knows how to obey:
       whether Master or Madam
       or Pharaoh or God,
A slave must obey.

I tried again:
       to obey,
       to do my duty,
       to raise a child.
But things had changed.
The child that was to be Sarai's
       now became my own responsibility,
But the jealousy and anger were still hers,
       and only she could bear them.

My son grew into a fine lad,
Ishmael, I called him:
       "God hears."
Fit and firm, as God had promised –
       'A wild ass of a man.'
Of course, wild asses don't make very good slaves –
       even Master Abram could see that,
Though he, too, loved Ishmael
       and considered him his own.

In time, Master Abram's God heard his plea, too,
       and granted him another son,
This one by Sarai.

The brothers loved each other,
       but that was also more than Sarai could bear:
She couldn't stand to see her son
       playing with the son of her slave,
So soon she sent us off again.

And I found myself in the desert again –
   this time with my son.

The sun beat fiercely against the sand.
The water Master Abram had sent with us
   soon ran out,
And there was nothing left for us.

Ishmael's fine firm body
   was no match for the scorching sun.
When he could walk no longer,
   I tried to carry him –
   though he was much too big for that now.
And then I laid him under a bush
   and went away.

A mother can bear her own sure death,
   but a mother cannot bear to watch her son die.

The sand had flowed through my fingers before
   like the days of our lives
   fleeting, burning, rushing to move on...
Now my tears made the sand
   clumped and matted in my hand,
A lifeless lump,
   no good to anyone.

When the tears had spent themselves
   I closed my eyes and prepared to die,
   obedient to the merciless sun overhead.

It was then that the Lord came to me again –
There in the scorching desert:
   the God who Sees and Hears and Heeds
   came to me again,
   and spoke to me.

God lifted me up and opened my eyes

to the spring of water before me.
God lifted me up and opened my eyes
        to see my son again,
And to see the hope that God offered!

God lifted me up and gave me water,
        gave me hope,
        gave me new life!

This, I tell you, is a different kind of God,
        a different kind of Master,
        a different kind of Pharaoh King:
This is a God who Sees and Hears and Heeds
        and Welcomes and Heals;
        who Loves and Watches over
        even a cast-out slave girl,
                and even her fatherless son.
This El-Roi! The God Who Sees!

Have you met this God?
        Do you know this God who see and hears and help?
Or are you too comfortable to cry out?

Do you know this God
        who listens to his servant?
Do you know this God
        who cares for those in great trouble?

I am an old woman now –
        A Hag, to be sure,
But a Holy Hag:
        one who has seen and heard and heeded
        the Holy One
                Who Sees and Hears and Heeds and Helps.

And I will tell you today:
        this God is ready and willing to help you, too,
Wherever you are,

    whatever your circumstances,
    whenever you call for help.
Amen.
May it be so with you.

TAMAR
(Genesis 38; Matthew 1:3)

Oh! Hello! Not often that I have visitors!
Have you come to see the twins?
They're sleeping now. Shh!
They were such restless babies
      and now that they're toddlers,
      they just wear themselves out!
They wear me out, too – but after all the years of waiting,
      it feels good to be tired out!

Here, sit a while:
You bless me by your presence
      as God has blessed me with the presence of the twins.
They are a special gift, you know:
      a promise fulfilled by El-Shaddai,
The God who hears the cry of the outcaste
      and acts on our behalf!

Surely, you've heard a bit of my story – everyone has!
      otherwise, why would you come?
I'm glad you've come to hear it from me:
What do the others know of what is and was in my heart?

And surely, you've heard of Judah, too, mighty Judah!

13

'Roaring like a lion,' that's Judah!
You've heard the echoes of his roar, no doubt,
        wherever you've come from.

But roaring doesn't mean right,
And Judah's stories of his God, El-Shaddai,
        who brought Judah's people
                from nothingness to multitudes,
                from barrenness to blessing,
The stories Judah told hinted that El-Shaddai didn't need to roar
        to be heard
        to be just
        to be holy.

The El-Shaddai God that we Canaanites heard about:
The God who heard the pleas of Sarah and of Hagar
        and Rachel and Leah and Rebekah,
The God who blessed them:
        that God was bigger than the roaring of Judah.

So, we let Judah roar and demand his 'due'
        and we looked beyond –
Beyond the rumours
        that Judah had sold his own brother into slavery,
        that he had come to our land to find a Canaanite wife
        because no Hebrew woman would have him.

Anyway, our Shua became his wife.
        Bore him three sons – what more could he want?
And then, following the example of Shua's father,
        my father agreed
        for me to become Judah's daughter-in-law.

I don't know about the others,
        but El-Shaddai seemed a better bet than our God, Baal.
So, I balanced the roaring of the man
        with the blessing of his God,
        and I became Judah's first daughter-in-law, Er's wife.

But from sour grape vines come sour grapes,
And Er had learned well his father's roar.
　　　too well.
The man was – evil!
　　　so evil that I cried out to El-Shaddai:
"Save me! Even if it means I am to be a widow,
　　　save me from this man!"

And the Lord heard my cry and answered me.

When Er was struck down dead,
I shivered in the presence of the Holy One of Israel.

Judah then looked on me with some suspicion:
　　　had this Canaanite woman cursed his son?
But Judah knew his duty then, and he did it:
　　　Judah sent Onan to me:
Onan, his second son,
　　　whose duty it was to fulfil his brother's line.

But Onan had also learned the evil ways
　　　of looking out only for his own –
He poured his seed onto the barren ground
　　　instead of into my fertileness:
No regard either for his brother's line
　　　or his brother's wife.

And the Lord struck him dead, too,
　　　before I could even dare to pray for deliverance!
So, Judah's second son was no more
And Judah's grief
　　　tore his roar
　　　into silence.
Stony silence.

A wall of narrow-eyed fear and distrust
　　　set between us.

Judah sent me away then,
>> sent me to be a widow in my father's house,
Telling me to wait for his third son,
>> whom we both knew would never come.

So I went – what choice did I have? –
I went back to my father's house,
>> a shamed widow
>> bringing shame to the whole household
Where the men glared their disgust at me
>> while the women made their desperate sacrifices
>> to Ashterah lamenting my barrenness.

I could not join the women
But lay numb in my shadowy corner
>> too exhausted to sleep
>> too famished to eat
>> too weary to think;
>> trying only to grasp a memory
>> of what hope I had found in Judah's God.

How many days or Sabbaths or moons passed by
>> I do not know.
Only that one day I heard a whispered voice
>> through the window
>> telling me that Shua, Judah's wife, had died.
From my fog I heard the women wailing
>> and then the silence.

Slowly, oh so slowly,
>> emerging from my dreamless stupor
I began to recognise a pinpoint of light
>> like a single star on a thick clouded night.
And I woke to view Abraham's sky
>> gleaming with the countless stars
>> of El-Shaddai's promise,
A promise to bless more than we could imagine.

16

Judah was now free:
>> available ... to marry again.

But a man willing to sell his own brother
>> surely would not stoop to redeem his son's widow.
>> to make matters right,
>> to do his duty.

But I might go to him.
I might use his blindness
>> to help him see:

I might use his disregard for women
>> to bring about regard for one woman.

The roaring of lions in the wilderness
>> echoed through my body.
For several tossing turning nights.
>> my belly wretched into knots,
And yet the gleeful justice of it all
>> would not leave me be.

So, when the news drifted through the open window
>> that Judah was bringing his sheep into town for shearing,
My body acted without conscious thought.

The body which he had discarded
>> wrapped itself in a new garb.
The face he had removed from his sight
>> shrouded itself in a veil.

For the first time in my life,
I became the tall, graceful palm tree
>> that my name suggests...
As I waited by the side of the road
>> at the entrance to our village.

I didn't have to wait long for him to arrive,

nor did I have to wait for him to speak to me.
I hoped that if he could see my smile behind the veil,
      he would think it hospitality
      instead of mirth,
For he, whose last word to me had been banishment,
      was now suggesting payment if I join with him!

It was hard not to snort at his 'offer':
      he offered as payment a kid from his flock.
How would a kid from his flock
      recompense the shame he had given me?
And how could I acknowledge his word as pledge?

No, what was just and right I asked for that day –
I demanded a guarantee:
      his signet on its cord
      and his staff.
His signet – the sign of all his patriarchal power,
And his staff — his very support and protection.
I asked for them,
      and El-Shaddai blessed me.
I trembled at the holiness in which they lay in my hand.

Then he lay with me.
      and then he was gone.
But the power and the protection I still held in my hand.

I hurried home,
      not really caring any more
      who would see.

Back in my widow's clothes,
      in my widow's corner,
I gathered the signet and the staff
      and hid them in the shadows.

A few days later there was much murmuring in town
      as Judah and his friend tried to locate

the cult prostitute to whom he owed his fare –
the kid from his flock –
Was it Ashterah's fertility cult he was seeking?
I bit my lip to hide my mirth.

Sometimes in the darkness,
I would take the signet and staff out from the shadows
        and hold them in my hand
And look out at the countless stars,
        and bless Judah's God, El-Shaddai.

It was on a dark early morning like that
        when I first felt the heaviness in my breasts
        and the swaying tide in my belly.
And after many puzzled moments,
I realised El-Shaddai's blessings
        had far exceeded my wildest dream:
There was life within me,
        and with that life, there was hope
        and a promise of blessing.

It was the retching that gave my widow's secret away.
        and soon word got to Judah
That his daughter-in-law —
        yes, now I suddenly was his daughter-in-law again
        and not merely a widow in my father's house! —
Judah's daughter-in-law was pregnant!

Good ol' roaring Judah!
Not enough to order me stoned:
        burning was his demand!
The women came to me with eyes wild,
        some wildly indignant at me,
        a few wildly believing in me,
        fewer still wildly grieving for me in silence.

El-Shaddai led my hand to the shadow,
        and the signet and staff emerged.

I placed them in another hand
      and told them to show these to Judah:
The signet and the staff belonged to the man
      whose child was within me.

The rest you know:
How Judah's eyes were finally opened
      to his own complicity in a system
      that had regard only for roaring
        instead of blessing.

How I was blessed!
Indeed, doubly blessed!
      with fine strong twin boys, Perez and Zerah,
      who were learning of sharing the blessings
        even as they tussled in my womb.

Judah's roaring is somewhat softer now.
He likes to see the boys:
      two sons gained for two sons lost!
But he's still a little afraid of me.
      He never comes to sleep with me.
But all the same, I'm blessed.
Not everyone, certainly not every woman,
      is so blessed.
Judah's sister, Dinah –
Ah, but that's another story,
      and the sun is getting low
      and soon the stars will be out...
You'd best be on your way.

Thanks for listening to me.
Telling the story helps.
It gives me hope that others, too,
      can find a way past the roaring
      into blessing.
Go in peace.

MIRIAM'S SONG
(Exodus 15:16-11; 20; 21)

I wasn't much of anybody before that day.
I was Moses' Big Sister, yes –
     and as the eldest sister, I was responsible enough.
After all, our mother had sent ME to watch Moses
     all those years ago
When the Pharaoh was trying to kill all the babies
     and we couldn't keep our precious little brother home
     any longer
     for fear of him crying out.

Mother had spent days making a basket –
     big enough for Moses' wriggling body,
     small enough that it wouldn't be too visible in the river,
     airy enough so he could breathe and see the sunlight,
     watertight so he'd stay afloat until...
Until what?
We didn't know.
We only knew we couldn't keep him safe with us anymore.
It would all be in God's hands.
Moses, our little brother,
     my little brother.
     the hope of our family.

I had watched and helped Mother make the basket,
     finding the right reeds,

soaking them,
  bending and weaving them together
      to make a tiny nest for him.
I was there when she whispered the prayers
      over the basket and the baby.
I was there, watching and waiting and listening
      to see and hear what God would do.

And then Mother looked straight at me
      and told me I was to stand watch!

At once I was proud—so proud she'd considered me worthy!
But also scared.
What would I do if something terrible happened?
      If the basket tipped over or started to leak?
      If a crocodile crept up?
      If one of Pharaoh's men walked by?

But Mother had given me the job,
      and we had prayed to God,
And now all my energy had to be focused on standing watch
      whether I was ready or not.

Well, you know the story:
How the Princess came by and spotted Moses in the basket.
How, in my panic, I blurted out the only thing I could think of:
      that I knew someone who could help.
Every fiber of my body was trembling,
But we had prayed, Mother and I,
      and somehow the words came out strong and true.
And soon Mother was telling me I had done just the right thing,
And that she thought the Power of the Lord was upon me!

In a real way, that was my initiation into womanhood,
      into adulthood.
I slowly began to see myself as someone God could —
      and would – use!
I knew the older women, my mother Jochebed,

and the Holy women: Shiphrah and Puah,
the midwives who helped my mother
and the other women
give birth to the babies and their dreams.
I knew them as women that God used powerfully
but also as ordinary women
who allowed God to use them
in extraordinary ways.

I saw others with talents,
but some of them seemed always full of fear;
they were afraid to do the things God called them to do.
I watched them shrivel up within themselves,
while others — perhaps less talented —
seemed to swell with usefulness
when they offered up their meagre talents.
Sometimes they seemed to explode with joy!

Moses was like that, too.
As proud as I had been of my little brother in the basket,
to see him grow up in the palace,
to keep watching him from afar:
I was very proud of what he was becoming!

But sometimes I was disappointed,
because I knew he had his faults as well –
a terrible temper sometimes,
and not always very sure of himself when he needed to be.
He wasn't very good at standing up to talk in front of others,
like our brother Aaron was.
But Moses did have a heart for his people,
and he loved God,
And he wanted to do what God asked,
even when what God required seemed quite impossible.

We all knew things were becoming quite impossible.
Pharoah and his men were SO cruel to us,
demanding we work and work

and produce more and more
Even as they kept decreasing our supplies
        and forcing us to work under harder conditions.

Still, we learned that when we were obedient
        to what GOD wanted,
        we somehow got Pharoah's jobs done, too.
But it was hard – too hard —
        and we all knew God had to do something
        to get us out of the awful situation.

Sometimes, in a quiet moment, I would find myself walking
        down to the side of the river,
And staring into the waters again,
        watching and waiting for God to act;
Trying again and again to be patient —
        not the easiest thing for one
        whose name means 'rebellious'!

Yet still I saw the others:
        that those who obeyed God's call
        were filled to the full
While the resisters shriveled up.

I watched as the locusts came
        with the frogs and the gnats and the flies,
        and the river's water turned to blood.
"Yahweh," I whispered,
        "Where are you in this chaos?"
The only answer that came was this:
        "Watch and wait and do what I tell you."

The watching and waiting seemed to last forever,
        but suddenly Moses gave us the signal,
And we all gathered together what we had,
        and what our neighbours gave us,
        and we left.

There was a miracle in that leaving, too,
        just as there had been a miracle in the Moses basket boat
            all those years before.
A miracle not just that we were able to leave,
        but that our neighbours gave us what we asked for!
I hadn't been too sure when Moses told us
        to ask our neighbours for money and clothes,
But I'd learned to put my misgivings aside
        and do the job given me.
And soon I was overflowing with gifts to take
        out of Egypt.

Out of Egypt!
So many still seem stuck in their own Egypts.
        Trapped, confined, overworked,
        mistreated, miserable.
I know that's not where God wants anyone to be.
Perhaps the stuck ones are still watching and waiting.
        for how God will lead them out.
I wonder if they know how to listen and embrace
        the strange and wonderful tasks God sets before them.
I wonder if they truly believe that they, too, can be free.

I do know what happened to us —
        to me and my sisters and brothers
        and all who loved and followed Yahweh.
We were set free.
        God's presence was with us.

There were still some scary times – some very scary times!
Like when Pharoah's huge chariots and horses
        were rushing down on us and forcing us into the sea!
But God was good and able
        using ordinary mud to trap the fancy chariots down.
        using extraordinary water piling up
            to let us walk across to safety,
            even as it then rushed down on our attackers.

I was beside myself with joy!
At a time like that, I couldn't sit quietly –
      I had to get up and dance and sing!
I found the tambourine that I'd packed away,
      and started singing and dancing
      right there in front of God and everybody.
No time for sitting and watching and waiting now
      God had acted!
No more waiting for someone else to go first.
No more waiting for the elders and important people to ask me.
I had seen it with my own eyes and felt it in my bones.
And I had acted as well!

At that point, I realized the waiting was over.
God's mighty power was here in our midst,
      getting me onto my feet and putting a song in my mouth.
Soon everyone else was singing as well
      and dancing and laughing and crying
      and hugging and kissing and embracing.
What else could we do?
After God had done all the hard work,
      were we going to sit quietly?
      What else were we waiting for?
No, it was the time to rejoice,
      the time to be fully alive in God's love.
Time to be re-created and join the creation in song;
      to leap into the dance,
No matter how ordinary our voice
      or how clumsy our feet.
With God's song on our lips
      we were all Extraordinary
      just as was the God who brought us through!

'I will sing unto the Lord,
      for he has triumphed gloriously,
The horse and rider thrown into the sea!
The Lord, my God, my Strength, my Song
      has now become my Victory!'

RAHAB
(Joshua 3)

Well, who have we here?
Welcome! You've come a long way
      to make it this far out of the settlement.
I guess you must be like me:
Living on the edge!

Have a seat.
Here, have some figs
      and some water from the well,
      and we can talk.
Surely, you've heard I like to talk!
When one lives on the edge,
      talking is a way of staying connected.
So, I talk,
      and if people don't want to listen,
      they can go back into town!

Actually, life out here
      at the edge of the settlement
      is not bad at all.
The Hebrew people treat me well,
      much better than my days on the edge of Jericho.

27

Here I'm a bit of a hero, I guess.
      There I was merely a harlot.

Funny how those titles come
      and stick to one like burrs in sheep's wool.

It was my hospitality that got me the harlot title:
A harlot in Jericho
      because I welcomed strangers.
A hero to the Hebrews
      because I welcomed their spies
      when they were strangers.

Somehow people think there was a choice involved:
That I chose to be a harlot:
      who would make such a choice?!?
That I chose to be a hero?
No, in both cases I chose only to welcome others
      and to survive.

There are few choices, you know,
      for the youngest daughter of a large and poor family.
Even in Mighty Jericho, the Great Walled City,
      there would be very few men left
      after the wars took them away each spring.
And those few who were left
      were prizes for the daughters of the rich men.
The oldest daughters first,
      and then the prettiest ones...
And after a while I realised
      that my options for marriage were very few.

I knew my family's flax trade well.
      I could spin and weave
      and make rope with the best of them:
          I was a spinster.
And when my brothers' wives and babies
      filled my father's house to overflowing,

28

I started building a little house of my own –
        just a room, really –
        in a place no-one else would claim.
I chose a spot on the wide city wall of Jericho.
I chose then to live on the edge.

You know, once you've made the decision,
        living on the edge is really an awesome adventure.
From the edge, one has a wonderful view
        of the respectable people
        living respectable lives
        inside respectable houses
        with respectable spouses
        and respectable children
        and respectable goats
        and respectable routines
        and respectable boredom.

But if you look over in the other direction,
You have a wonderful view of the rest of the world:
        howling desert and scorching sun
        and camels and mountains
        and palm trees and oases
        and travellers coming from all corners of the earth;
        traders trading,
        soldiers marching
        new friends who are only strangers
            because you haven't met them yet...

And so, you invite them in
        and become acquainted
        and sing new songs
        and hear new stories
        and laugh at new jokes.
And the respectable people
        look up from their respectable boredom
And wonder what there is to laugh about
        and decide it must not be anything respectable

And so, they label she-who-laughs-with-strange-men
        as a harlot.

Which, in a way, is a great relief,
        because then respectable people
                don't bother you anymore
And the adventurous ones find their way to you
        without bothering anybody else!

And so, I spent my days
        living on the edge,
Spinning my flax and linen and stories
        and laughing at jokes
        and hearing others' stories of a world beyond.

So it was that afternoon when those two young men came.
        Handsome men they were,
And I guessed before I heard them speak
        that finally the Hebrews had found their way
        out of the desert.

We'd heard stories of them for years!
Even before I moved to the wall,
        I'd heard of how their god had defeated Pharoah –
        just imagine!
And then more recently, the stories of King Sihon's trouncing
        and mighty Og's defeat filled the air with excitement.
Excitement and fear:
        fear of attack
        fear of war,
Especially for those whose respectability
        depended on their safety.
It was fear that built the Famous Walls of Jericho –
        thick wide double walls, one inside the other,
        wide walls that made would-be conquerors
                very reluctant to attack.

Of course, a house atop a wall

is not very safe in a war
At least not in the respectable context.
But my safety had always lay
      in my hospitality,
      in my ability to listen
      and learn from the stories of stranger.

Knowing my guests that day
      were scouts for people with a very powerful god,
I listened very carefully indeed,
      as I offered them dates and olives and goat's milk.
I listened carefully to hear if the stories rang true.

But as I listened, I heard something different
      in the way they talked about their god.
It was a radically different god
      than the ones I'd heard about before.
They talked about a god
      who pitied an enslaved people —
      the Hebrews!
And brought their ancestors –slaves – out of a foreign land —
      Mighty Egypt!

A god who was powerful,
      yet willing to act on behalf of slaves,
      on behalf of the lowest rung of society;
A god who was powerful
      even in a land where a Pharaoh reigned —
That must be a very different god indeed!

A god different than the local territorial deities
      which the respectable priests blessed
      so that they could keep their respectable priestdoms;
So different than the local gods
      who demanded sacrifices to keep the local city safe.

Perhaps this god who had power
      for unrespectable people

outside a local area:
This god might be a suitable god
      for those who lived on the edge
      even on the edge of mighty Jericho.

So, yes, I listened very hard
      to my guests that day,
And I decided such a god must truly be
      the God of Heaven and all the earth!
This was MY kind of God!

From that moment on,
      I never looked back over the respectable side of the wall,
Though I knew, of course,
      that the respectable side was looking up at me.,
      perched on the edge,
And that it would be no time at all
      before the respectable grapevine
      had speeded news of my guests to the king.
      (Gossip travels fastest in the most respectable places!)

By then I had hospitably shown my guests
      the abundant stack of flax on my roof,
And they were comfortably hidden away
      by the time the king's messengers arrived
      demanding I turn my guests over —
          over to the king!

Ah! Respectability demanding respect
      from despised Adventure!
I still had a length of flaxen rope in my hand
      from the roof,
And I gripped it hard
      to keep my face sober
      as I told the messengers that the Hebrew men
          had left my room... earlier...
And that they should hurry to overtake them.

As soon as the door was shut,
  and the sounds of their voices far down the road,
The laughter sputtered out from my lips
  scaring all the cats into the shadows.

When I could contain myself,
  I hurried upstairs and made my deal with the young men.
We peered over the edge into the darkness,
   the flaming torches of the running soldiers
   making eerie streaks in the distance.

We negotiated in whispers
   about how I would let them down
   with one of my ropes,
    the red one,
And to which hills they would escape
   and how long they should stay away.
And then we spoke of the oncoming attack from the Hebrews
   and we agreed that my red rope
   would hang again from the window
   on the edge,
Like the red blood on the Hebrew door frames
   during their Passover flight.

As my red rope would save their lives,
   so it could save mine,
   and it could save the lives of my family
Assuming that, for once,
   my family would attempt a Lifegiving Adventure
   instead of a fatal respectability.

And so the men slipped away that night
   from the edge
   on my rope
   into a blanket of night.

Several days later
   my rope saved the lives of my family and myself as well.

I was the last one down
     from my house on the edge
Before the wall fell
     in a deafening, deadly crash,
followed by screaming and wailing
     as the respectable ones
        all went up in flames.

Oh my people, don't you know
     that walls won't keep you safe?
I took away with me
     a length of my rope
To help me remember
     those days on ethe edge
And the God who welcomes harlots
     into the clan
and makes them into heroes.
==
You know, it's hard for a hero
     to live on the edge.
Everybody wants to think of a hero as
     respectable.
I think God understands that:
     win a few wars,
     rescue a few slaves,
     and they even want to turn God into a king.
Somehow, I don't think God wants to be a king.
     How would a king live on the edge?

But I am an old woman now.
     Somehow, I'm respectable enough to have a husband!
A Hebrew man
     who still has enough desert sand in his sandals
     to resist too much respectable safety.

I have a son, too:
     Boaz – a fine, handsome young man
     who grows barley instead of flax,

But I tell him to watch out for – and protect –
      the young women who work in his field,
      especially the ones who live on the edge:
"In the name of the God who lives on the edge,
      Look out for them, Boaz!"

Someday he'll probably marry too;
      respectability has a great pull to it!

I'm sure you've found that out for yourself—
And you're probably ready for this old woman
      to stop talking so you can go home:
Go home to safety and respectability.

As for me, I'll keep holding on to my red rope
      and watching the adventure from the edge
You're most welcome to join me if you'd like.
There's always room for one more
      in the adventure.
Me and my rope
      and my totally unrespectable God,
We like here on the edge.
      Perhaps you'd like to join us.

RUTH
(Ruth)

Naomi gone?
How could that be?
I guess I just need to say it over and over
       until I get used to it.

Naomi is dead.
People I loved have died before.
       That's nothing new.
People die all the time!
       But we never get used to it...

Grief: it's such a strange thing,
       such a hard thing.
They said I should have grieved more when Mahlon died.
Well, I did grieve in my own way,
       but I didn't know much about grieving,
       and we had only been together such a short time.
And Naomi is – was – such an expert griever,
       that the rest of us pretty much left it to her:
       to do the grieving for the rest of us.

But if Naomi is gone...
       Who will do my grieving if I don't do it myself?

Some people grieve silently.
That wasn't Naomi's way.
What she would do is talk.
      Remember.
That's it: re-member
      remember the past
      to bring it back into focus,
      so, the present would make more sense.

Naomi, I'll re-member today.

They all warned me before I married
      what a mother-in-law would be like.
How she would be jealous of me
      for taking her son,
How she would treat me harshly
      as her mother-in-law had done to her
      and as I would someday do to my daughter in-law.
And since I was a Moabite
      and she was a Hebrew,
They told me it would be even worse,
      since Hebrews hated Moabites,
And the only reason to marry one
      was to ensure the male line continued.

But somehow it wasn't like that with us.
      Naomi never meant anyone any harm.
Indeed, she was more of a mother to me
      than my own mother.
And I became her daughter.

More than that:
      we became friends.
I needed her wisdom;
      she needed my vigour.
She talked; I listened.
She planned; I did.

She plotted for safety and security;
  I chose risk.
She decided with her head;
  I decided with my heart.

It didn't really hit me how much we needed each other
  until she was ready to leave Moab.
I guess we were all in a fog then,
  still reeling from the deaths
  of Elimelech and Mahlon and Chilion.
Terrified to think what would become of us:
  three widowed women with no men
  to support or protect us.

But the moment it came into her head
  to go back to Bethlehem,
  I knew I would go, too.
It didn't make any sense, they said.
What hope was there for me,
  a widowed, childless, Moabite woman
  in Bethlehem?

Actually, Orpah and I both followed her
  as far as the Jordan.
And then Naomi, the practical one,
  told us to go back.
She told us she wouldn't last long:
  Go back to the fertile land of Moab
  where we had a future...

Orpah did go back,
  and we missed her cheerful spirit those first few days.
Naomi still tried to talk me out of following,
  but she soon gave up.
Even then, we knew each other well enough
  to each know I would follow her wherever.
And so, we continued on our journey.

In the beginning we had shared memories
      and shared grief.
But as we went along,
      we began to share the journey, too.
How we survived I'll never know.
      over rivers and streams
      up mountain and down,
Naomi's feeble legs weak,
      "One more step, Naomi-ma," I'd tell her:
      "Soon we'll be in the Promised Land!"

Ah! The stories she'd tell me about the Promised Land!
      I know she'd never have left her beloved Israel
      if it hadn't been for the famine.
But Moab, with its reputation for fertility,
      what had it gotten her?
A full belly, perhaps,
      but it emptied her womb
And her arms...
      and mine...?

The Moabite god, Chemosh, had not been friendly to me.
      Why should I remain in his land?
Naomi's word – about El-Shaddai's Promised Land –
      was all I needed to believe.

So, we trudged together through wilderness
      and slept in haystacks
      and ate whatever we could find.
The sun was hot,
      and the night was cold,
But we had each other,
      and we surprised ourselves
To find that woman could be friend
      with woman.

The journey took its toll on her.
I often woke early and would check first

to see if she breathed still.
I never imagined what I would do
        if she stopped breathing...
Never till today...

She was tired then.
        She ached.
        She got depressed.
        She complained.
But Naomi, my friend,
        was always still breathing in the morning.

And so, we would start another day together.
She would give thanks to El-Shaddai
        and ask for protection for the day.
I would mumble along,
        wondering what kind of God
        could really be worshipped so...

And at the end of the day,
        she would give thanks again
And we would lay down and sleep
        while her God watched over us.

When we finally got to Bethlehem,
        it didn't take her long to make a plan.
She sent me out to the fields,
        and I was glad to have some work to do.
She had warned me that the Hebrews
        would think me a wanton woman
        being a Moabite,
So I watched the others carefully
        out of the corner of my eye
And tried to remember all Naomi had taught me
        about how the Hebrews did things.

Her plan worked!
There was work to do and food to eat –

armloads of barley!
And very little time to think back to Moab.

The next thing I knew, I was even eating
      with the owner of the field...
He was a handsome man,
      ah, yes, you know Boaz –
Such a good man!
It was more than I could fathom
      that he would become our *go-el*,
      the kinsman-redeemer for both Naomi and me —
And more than that,
      a husband for me!

I think Naomi must have had the whole thing
      planned out from the beginning.
She knew I was good at seizing the moment,
      so she worked hard to make sure
      the moments were there to be seized.
And so I seized a husband,
      a good man
      who took care of both of us, Naomi and me.
A man through whom God blessed my womb
      with a son.
      A son to continue Elimelech's line.
      A son to warm Naomi's arms.
      A son to melt the knots in her heart
         as she had melted mine.

I re-member, Naomi!
      I re-member you!
Thank you for the memories;
      they help me grieve a little now.
==
The wailers from town have come and gone.
      Boaz paid them well.
      and they did a proper job of it.
But what do they know of the worth of a woman,

a woman worth being friends with?
What do they know of love that has no explanation?
The wailers wailed with such ferociousness —
      as if El-Shaddai would only hear
      the Thunder
           instead of the gentle rain.

Good-bye, Naomi.
      Sleep peacefully, my friend.
I promised long ago
      that your people would be my people
      and your God would be my God
      and your tomb would be my tomb.

Someday I'll join you there, Naomi.
Until then,
Sleep well, my love.

DANCING WITH HANNAH
(1 Samuel 1:4-20; 2 Sam 2:1-10)

Hannah, my sister!
Hannah, my mother!
How much I have to learn from you!

I, too, have had those around me
      who seem to overflow with blessings.
You had Peninnah –
      full to overflowing with an endless issue of children –
So full of herself
      that she couldn't see your pain,
Or if she did, your pain seemed to somehow satisfy her.
Perhaps she despaired privately with all those children –
      but she couldn't breathe a word of that to you –
The only salve she knew for her discomfort
      was to make things worse for you...

How did you bear it, year after year?
I imagine it was almost bearable during the ordinary times.
You had your duties to keep you busy:
      a husband to tend,
      a house to maintain –
         simpler to do with fewer bodies around!

But then would come the Holiday Times
When families were paraded, and children abounded
        from every womb but yours.
How did you face the time of other's abundance?

Did your poverty seem particularly painful then?
        Did you want to scream out?
        or hide away?

Today I'm thanking you, Hannah,
        for going with the rest to the temple.
        for taking your place at the table with dignity,
        for being there with the others
                when you really didn't feel like it.

I'm thanking you today, Hannah, for your prayers.
I'm thanking you for reminding me to go to God
        with my problems,
To not being afraid to tell the Most Holy One
        of my Most Lowly and Lonely Thoughts.

I'm thanking you for having the guts to respond to Eli.
        He was such a high and holy man
        that you could have slunk away into the night,
Not only bereaved by your loss,
        but bruised by his words.

I thank you for refuting him.
It wasn't wine you had poured out
        but your own heart,
        your own despair.
I thank you for recognising in yourself
        a vessel that God loved,
                even if God had kept you empty for so long.

I'm thanking you for reminding me to pour myself out,
        because sometimes that's the only way
        there will be enough room

for God to be poured into me.

I'm thanking you for insisting
        not so much on your own way –
        on what you could get or be by way of status –
But for recognising the gift you received
        as something you could return to God
        and not just hold tightly for yourself:
A son who would not remain your own
        but a son who, as a gift, you could return to God.

Thank you for that insistence, Hannah:
        for reminding me that what God gives me
        is not for me to keep
        but for me to share.
For reminding me that gifts are not to retain –
        like the Dead Sea
        continually absorbing the Jordan River's bounty
        but never emptying itself into another body –
                until it becomes rank and acrid,
                unable to support any life —
        but as a flowing stream
        receiving and giving and receiving again.
I thank you, Hannah, for being a vessel
        that could receive
        and could give back
                and thus renew the lives of us all.

You are a gift to me, Hannah.
        I am proud to call you my mother.
==
And now today, dear Hannah, I also want to thank you
        for reminding me about the dance.
I might have forgotten,
        if you hadn't taken the time and effort
To put it into words
        that won't leave me alone.

•

I know what you mean about "dancing your salvation;"
      sometimes, I, too, am just so full of God
      and God's unexpected love for me
That I want to leap and twist and turn in the air
      full of love and laughter and energy –

Those are the times when – suddenly –
      the loneliness and everyday fears,
      the misery and monotony are wiped away –
And I can see how God was there all the time –
      like the sun —
      just hidden behind the shadows I had allowed to fall on my path...

Sometimes the dance is slower and more refined;
      sometimes my salvation dance is more concerned
      with putting one foot in front of the other.
My aches and pains make movement difficult
      and yet I'm still vaguely aware of moving forward –
Getting closer and closer to the fullness of my salvation –
      the Me that God really intended from the very beginning...

Some days my dance is high and mighty;
      Some days it is low and subdued.
Some days I have more than I can use,
      and I'm full to overflowing!
Other days, I have just enough
      and the dance is even sweeter for its simplicity.

I'm thankful that the dance of my salvation is not always the same –
      I would get dull with too much dazzle
And if I was always in the lead,
      it would be too easy to forget the joy of following along
      and learning the path another has discovered
      and wants to share with me.

I'm thankful, too, Hannah,
      that your dance includes me across the ages.
I thank you that you've danced God's dance in the past

and are showing me the way today.

I'm thankful that there are others to dance with.
      Sometimes a solo dance is nice,
But the best dances are when everyone can join in:
      a big circle dance with room enough for all.

And so I'm wondering today, Hannah:
      Shall we invite Peninnah to the dance?

RIZPAH

(1 Samuel 31:10; 2 Samuel 3:1, 6-7; 4:12; 21:1-14, 22-23; Psalm13:1-20;
Deuteronomy 21:23)

Ah! Rizpah!
Daughter of Aiah,
A concubine of King Saul.
Lest we look down our noses at 'concubine,'
      we're reminded that 'concubine to the King'
        was a high as a slave woman could go in ancient times.
Very beautiful, very blessed.

Two sons she bore to King Saul,
      Armoni and Mephibosheth,
Royal heirs:
      Pride of their father,
      Hope of their mother.

But, ah! Rizpah!
      The life of a concubine was not all sweetness!
The death of her husband Saul
      meant she became a pawn in power struggle
      between Ishbosheth and Abner --
Fighting over who was to succeed Saul,
      each claiming Rizpah as their own,
      in the fight for ultimate power:
Fighting until they were both killed as well.

Ah, Rizpah,
        widowed concubine,
Discarded finally by King David,
        seeking to rid himself of Saul's house
Left with only her sons by which to claim her place.
Rizpah: older, wiser,
        no longer in demand,
        disappearing from the picture for a while.
        Silent. Forgotten.

Then disaster strikes the whole of the land,
        as it does from time to time:
Famine! Drought!
The world staring directly into the face of death
        as nature's fatal fury unleashed:
        floods, tornadoes,
        wildfires flaring out of control;
        private insulated and isolated worlds
            turned upside down.
All crying out: "Who's to blame?"
So King David cried out for Judah:
        Whose responsibility is this, God?
        Who's to pay?
        Who's to blame for disaster?

The answer comes that Saul's house must pay:
David must pay the foreigners, the Gibeonites,
        to be rid of the drought –
Pay to remove the blood guilt on their land,
        guilt incurred by Saul.

What price would the Gibeonites demand?
We don't want money, they replied:
        lives were taken.
        lives are required.
An eye for an eye, tooth for tooth,
        a wound for a wound.
Seven sons of Saul required

to repay the bloodguilt of Saul:
The sins of the father
    visited on the second and third generations.

Except, there weren't seven sons of Saul left.
    Jonathan, Ishbosheth, and their two brothers
        were all dead.
There were still two sons of Saul left: Rizpah's sons,
    and Saul's five grandsons: Merab's sons,
And these become the vicarious sufferers,
    to fulfill the royal cleansing of communal guilt
    for Saul's house,
So that God's anger would be appeased,
    and the drought would end,
    and life would go on.

And so, on the first day of the barley harvest,
The seven 'sons' of Saul were sacrificed
    'on the mountain of the Lord.'
    Hanged? Impaled?
    'Flung down the mountain of the Lord'?
The grisly truth of their deaths
    too gruesome for language to reveal,
And yet, not as grisly as what followed.

For David's actions spoke louder than his words:
If the death were really to propitiate guilt,
    to bring about an end to the drought,
Then David would certainly have known
    that the bodies had to be buried.

As the Law of Deuteronomy states:
"If a man has been put to death for a crime
    and his body is hung on a post,
It is not to remain there overnight.
It must be buried the same day,
    Because a dead body hanging on a post
    brings God's curse on the land.

Bury the body,
> so that you will not defile the land
> that the Lord your God is giving you."

But David left the bodies there on the mountain,
> exposed,
> on display,

As the body of Saul had been nailed
> to the wall of the city of Beth Shan.

As the hand and feet of Rechab and Baanah had been cut off
> and hung up near the pool in Hebron
> after they had killed Ishbosheth, Saul's son.

No, if David had really intended
> to remove the blood guilt from the land,
> he wouldn't have left the bodies exposed.

His intentions were screaming loudly:
> "This is not about cleansing the land,
> this is about revenge,
> about establishing power and authority:
> MY reign, not Saul's."

Actions shouting louder than words.

But while David's actions screamed, 'Disgrace,'
> Rizpah's silent actions proclaimed 'Grace.'

Ah, Rizpah,
> whose husband, Saul, had been beheaded,
> whose subsequent would-be masters were slaughtered,
> and whose sons and step-grandsons were now
> > not only dead
> > > but disgraced...

Rizpah comes in silence
> to sit on the mountain for five long months.

In mourning she takes sackcloth
> and spreads it on a rock for herself.

She performs a praxis of presence:

being there, being in solidarity:
a silence that shouts at the injustice,
a lifestyle that demands an explanation.
Enough is enough.

Rizpah sits in silence
in that shadowy land
where life communes with death,
where vultures seek to further the transformation
of dust to dust.
Rizpah sits in silence
doing grief work,
finding a routine, a structure to handle the chaos:
Caring for dead bodies.
Bodies that stink as they swell
and turn from green to blue to black.
Keeping the vultures and wild animals away:
Shoo! Shoo!
As the skin dries into leather
till only bones are left.
Dry bones.

Rizpah's lips silently recall the Psalm:
"How much longer will you forget me, Lord?
How much longer will you hide yourself from me?
How long must I endure trouble?
How long will sorrow fill my heart, day and night?
How long will my enemies triumph over me?"

Ah! Rizpah!
Her name means 'glowing stone,'
like the rock she sat on?
like the glowing stones
that baked Elijah's 'arise and eat' cake?
like the glowing coals that cleansed Isaiah's lips?

Rizpah – glowing stones to cleanse?
to strengthen?

to cleanse the land of blood guilt?
to re-member those senselessly killed?
to mourn the death of dreams?
to hear voices silenced?
to proclaim through action that God hears?

Rizpah sits in a shouting silence,
        a presence demanding a response.
Waiting silently for the disgrace to be over,
        for the respect of a proper burial,
Not just the bones of her sons and grandsons
        but the bones of Saul, too...

Had Rizpah seen Saul beheaded?
        Surely she had heard the tales.
        Surely she knew where his bones were.
        Surely she knew whose responsibility it was.
Rizpah's silence shouting out to David:
        "These bones are mine to watch over,
        but they are yours to bury!"

After five long months
        of the Glowing Stone
                sitting in silence on the mountain,
David heard.
And he took the bones of Saul and Jonathan
        with those from the mountain
        and buried them in the tomb of Saul's father, Kish.

And then the rains came
        to cleanse the guilt,
        to make the land fertile again
Fertility returned through cleansing blessings
        of rain and of tears.

Rizpah's job was finished.
God heard.
God blessed.

God healed,
        Not just the land
                But the heart.
==
There are other Rizpahs who sit and watch and remember
        broken dreams and promises:
Mothers of untraced victims,
Children who have disappeared,
Three Marys at a tomb.

Shall we sit with them
        and weep
        and remember?
Help them name the grief,
        mourn the loss,
        keep the memory and the pain alive,
        until the bones can be buried,
        until the pain can be healed?

Shall we join the shouting silence:
        "God hears,
        God remembers,
        God weeps with us.
        God hears. God heeds, God heals"?

Shall we find the wounded parts of ourselves
        that need to sit and weep?
Have we done our own grief work?
        Named our grief?
        Buried the bones?

We sit with Rizpah, the glowing stone,
        high up on the mountain,
And wait in the presence of the One
        who hears and heeds and remembers,
For the time when the rains will come
        and heal the heart
        And cleanse the land again. Amen.

BATH-SHEBAH
(2 Samuel 11, 12; Proverbs 31)

My name is Bath-Shebah:
      Daughter of an Oath.
Perhaps you know me by other names:
      Mother Of Solomon,
      Queen Mother,
      Wife of King David,
      Wife of Uriah the Hittite.
I am all of these and more,
But mostly I am Bath-Shebah:
      Daughter of an Oath.

An oath is a powerful thing.
An oath is Word Spoken,
      Promise Given,
      Trust fulfilled.

Trust is a strange thing.
      "Trust in the Lord with all your heart
      and lean not on your own understanding."
Trust I've struggled with,
      perhaps because of my name,
      perhaps because of my story.
Trust must be earned.
Slowly I've learned to trust the Lord.

Of course, some say that my name, 'Shebah,'
      refers to the beautiful and fertile land of Shebah.
Perhaps.

My husbands called me 'beautiful.'
My sons, Solomon and Shimea and Shobab and Nathan,
      Call me 'wise.'
Yet wisdom can be trusted
      While beauty made me a victim.

I was young then,
The young bride of Uriah the Hittite,
      a good man, a strong man,
        one of King David's Thirty Famous Soldiers.
Uriah had gone off to fight for King David
      and I missed him very much.

I was bathing that day,
      the ritual cleansing after my monthly period.
I wanted to keep myself clean and pure
      for Uriah,
Trusting he would return home from battle,
      but never knowing when.
My oath of faithfulness I had given to Uriah.

King David's palace
      was above us on the eastern ridge of Jerusalem.
King David was very powerful in those days.
Can one trust power?
      He had not gone to fight in this battle.
      He had plenty of men to fight for him.
He also had plenty of women in the palace,
      at least three wives and many concubines, they said.

But that afternoon,
      he looked down from his palace roof,
And saw my beauty
      and ignored my oath.
King David sent messengers to bring me to him.
One did not refuse a message from the king,
      so I went with them.
And they took me to his bedroom

and there King David raped me.

With his weight on top of me,
      all I could think of was my beloved Uriah
Out on another battlefield,
      and how I would never be clean again.
I would bathe and bathe again and again,
      but I would never be clean for Uriah again.
David had stolen Bath-Shebah's oath.

David sent me home
      when he was finished with me.
As I bathed my body time and again,
      my tears bathed my face
      and tried in vain to bathe my soul.
I cried out to the Lord for help.
The Torah said that the punishment for adultery
      was death by stoning.
In this case, that was the price for being beautiful
      and trusting the king for protection.
I prayed to the Lord that those in David's palace
      would keep their royal secret.
A king would not be killed for adultery,
      especially a powerful king like David.
As long as I stayed silent
      perhaps my life would be spared as well,
At least the part of my life
      that was still alive.

But my body would not remain silent.
      My stomach began to churn.
      My belly began to swell.
Everyone knew Uriah was not at home,
      and everyone would soon hear my body
      screaming its shame.
My screaming body would shame
      my dear Uriah.
And there would be no other option

except that I would be put to death.

I prayed to the Lord for pardon, for help,
      and I waited for what would come next.

It was during the waiting
      that the Lord sent a gift.
I tell my sons, "A gift from the Lord can be trusted."

The Lord sent to me a long-time family friend,
      Nathan, from the royal palace;
      Nathan, whose name means 'gift;'
      Nathan the Prophet,
          trusted by both the king and the harem;
      a gift I knew I could trust as well.
Nathan knew my story.
      Nathen knew my Uriah.
      Nathan knew David,
      and Nathan knew the Lord.
Nathan was not afraid of truth,
      and he taught me how to trust again.

Nathan helped me see another option:
      a woman sentenced to death
      has nothing else to fear.

So, I spoke in words
      what my body was screaming.
I sent the king a message.
      Two words: "I'm pregnant."

I waited again after that.

I thought one day I saw Uriah at the palace gate,
      but I could not go out in my condition.
And I knew Uriah would not come to me
      While the rest of the soldiers were fighting.

A strange present from the palace
        arrived at my house soon after,
But Uriah did not arrive.

And then one day
Nathan sent the message
        that Uriah had been killed in battle.
Some said that David had arranged for him
        to be killed on the front lines,
And that Uriah
        had carried his own death warrant
                to Joab, the general!

From the depth of my body
        came wave after wave
        of grief and rage.
I wept for the husband I would no longer have.
I wept for all the brave, righteous men
        fighting senseless wars for kings.
I wept for the innocents
        and all those treated unjustly.
And I wept for myself
        and the child I was carrying.
I wept for days and days,
        until there were no more tears.

King David then sent for me,
        gathering me in like his harvest.
And he took me for his wife.

The days passed in a blur.
Suddenly I had position and power
        as the king's wife,
When all I wanted was quiet
        and home with Uriah.

My final months of confinement
        were spent in the harem

Where the confusion of scheming competition
        mirrored the turmoil
        inside my body and soul.

And then the baby was born.
A son, yes, but a sickly child
        carrying in his innocent body
        all the rage and anger and shame
        that had smothered my world
        for those past nine moons.

Part of me loved that child fiercely
        and another part loathed the sight of him.

Through the haze, I heard of the story
        that Nathan told David,
A story of a 'lamb like a daughter,'
        like a 'bath.'
And I knew the story was about me,
        but it was as if it were another person in another story.

I also heard that king David had repented.
        Was that possible?
        that a king would – could - admit his guilt?
A small part of me knew
        that the Lord had heard my prayers
        and my grief
        and my anger
        and had sent Nathan and his story
As a gift to me
        and to women everywhere and at every time
        who are used, abused, discarded.

A part of me was grateful
        but the larger part of me was numb,
So much so that,
When the baby died,
        I couldn't think of any reason to live myself.

It was then that David came to comfort me.
In my stupor I sensed
        that perhaps his grief was real, too.
He had no idea of how to comfort me,
        except to lie with me again.
I was too numb to respond,
        and yet I felt a small bond
        of common humanity between us.

That seed of shared human grief
        grew slowly within me during the following months
Along with the small seed
        of another baby enlarging my womb.

When our son was born,
        David named him Solomon: Peace.
Though it was my place to name the child
        I took his naming as a peace offering.
I think it was the best he could do for me,
        and I accepted it as that,
        not Trust but Peace.

Though David named my son,
        I raised my son.
And I was determined to raise him in wisdom,
        in reverence for the Lord,
In respect for all the Lord's people
        and their dignity.

The years that followed were difficult ones in the palace.
David called for me often enough
        and three more sons I bore him.
As Chief Wife,
        I had respect in the harem,
And Nathan remained my trusted friend.

But David continually over-indulged his older sons,

And in the palace,
       rape and murder reigned:
            brother against brother.
            brother against sister.
It was a place of madness and distrust.
It was hard to raise good children there,
       but the Lord gave me strength day by day
       to raise my sons in the ways of wisdom,
       wisdom I knew would serve them well all their days.

As David continued to call for me
       I gradually began to believe
       that perhaps he did love me.
I would catch glimpses of a very human soul
       secretly longing to be rid
       of the weight of the king's mask.
Sometimes he would read to me
       one of his psalms.
And I would recite for him the wisdom proverbs
       my mother and grandmothers had taught me.
I believe he began to trust
       my womanly wisdom
Even as my youthful beauty faded.

My Solomon, too, David respected.
Once David even swore to me
       that Solomon would succeed him to the throne.
I dared not breathe a word of David's oath
       to anyone but Nathan.

In time, David's youth faded, too.
And it was well known that a king without sexual power
       was a king without political power.
When even young and beautiful Abishag
       was unable to spark David's powers,
The palace became a beehive of competition
       for the throne.

Living in that blood-thirsty melee of mistrust,
Each one of us knew that to lose the throne
      was to chance one's life as well.
Having faced certain death before
      I hardly considered my own risk any longer,
But Solomon's life was different.
And indeed, all of Israel deserved
      the reign of peace and wisdom
      that he offered.

Nathan encouraged me,
      as he had so many times before.
He went with me to speak to David
      about Solomon's succession to the throne.

Through the gift of Nathan, I had learned
      how to risk – beyond trust!
      How to speak.
I knew that the time for me to speak was at hand.
I knew how David thought
      and what he feared.
I knew that his son Adonijah,
      crowning himself King
      with all his chariots and horsemen and soldiers,
Actually anticipated trouble.
That by ignoring me and my son,
      he feared wisdom and truth and peace

And so I went into David's bedroom.
I reminded King David of his Oath,
      his Shebah in the name of the Lord.
      his Oath that Solomon would be king.
Afterwards Nathan came in to confirm my story.
Then David did renew his Oath
      and Solomon became king.

David died soon after,
      but the troubles continued.

Adonijah still tried to oust Solomon.
Solomon, despite his reputation for wisdom,
        sometimes, like his father before him,
        could only see blood revenge as a solution.
How many generations would it take
        for wisdom and peace and trust to prevail?

At Solomon's first wedding
I presented him with a collection of Wisdom sayings:
        "To have knowledge,
        you must first have reverence for the Lord.'

'Son, when sinners tempt you,
        saying, 'let's find someone to kill,'
        don't give in.
Stay away from people like that
        who are always ready to kill."

I told Solomon to protect and speak up
        for people who could not speak for themselves.
I, who had found my voice,
        knew how difficult that finding could be.
So I told him to speak for those without a voice,
        to be a righteous judge,
        to protect the rights of the poor and needy.

"Trust in the Lord with all your heart.
        Never rely on what you think you know.
Remember the Lord in everything you do,
        and the Lord will show you the right."

Now I am an old woman,
And I hear the scribes
        reading the Wisdom Proverbs attributed to Solomon;
"Never forget what you mother taught you."
        "Charm is deceptive,
        and beauty disappears
        but a woman who honours the Lord should be praised.

Give her credit for all she does.
>She deserves the respect of everyone."

My name is: Bath-Shebah;
>Daughter of an Oath,
>Word Spoken,
>Promise Given,
>Still trusting that the Lord will fulfil.

ELIZABETH'S SILENCE
(Luke 1)

Welcome to the silence.
Is there a part of you that knows silence?
      that knows barrenness?
      that can hear in the speechlessness of it all?
They used to call me the Silent One.
A priestly house is often silent
      especially when there are no children around.
A priestly house knows reverence.
Sacred space.

Sometimes I would go to the wilderness
      just to hear the wind rushing.
Other days I would go into town,
      into the bazaar – full of noise:
            Sellers shouting their wares.
            Buyers haggling over prices.
            Camels snorting.
            Goats bleating.
            Children laughing and crying.
Alive with noise,
      alive with life.
Sometimes I would just stand,
      fascinated by the noise,
      the confusion,
      the turmoil.

I would wonder:

> Is there a quiet centre for these people?
> What noise do they go home to?
> Where is their silence?

Sometimes I ached for the noise, too,
My silent womb so stubbornly refusing
> to add to the hubbub of life.
But a barren womb
> does not mean a barren soul.

In the beginning it was painful,
> especially during the festival times
When all the family would come to our house
> to celebrate in Jerusalem.
So painful,
> to be the one with the silent womb
> amid the celebration of life.
After a while,
> the silence became my shield,
> my protection from the onslaught of the outside noise.

In my silence
> I could walk among the others
> but still hear into the silence,
My barren womb
> giving space for the voice of God:
Showing me which one needed help,
> which one was hurting inside,
> which one was unable to say
> what was inside her heart.

I began to understand God had birthed in me
> an understanding of silence,
And I held that creation of silence
> carefully in my arms,
> In my heart,

And nurtured it
>   as the gift from God that it was.

Elizabeth, you call me,
>   Elisheba, my original name:
>   Oath of God, God's Promise,
>   an oath to revere silence.
Elisheba was the name of Aaron's wife as well,
>   and so I inherited a priestly function, too.
Sometimes I thought that my gift of silence
>   was ordination for fulfilling the duties of
>   Wife of the Priest.
I had time and space for listening to
>   the Holy One of Israel,
For hearing the joys and troubles of Zechariah,
>   my husband, the priest.

I think we shared more than the other couples,
>   Zechariah and me;
We shared because we only had each other.
He did not try to throw me out
>   because I was barren.
Perhaps he knew, too,
>   the pregnant silence within me
And knew the hallowed meaning
>   of that sacred space.
It was a space that accommodated his speech.
How he loved to talk!
>   He talked enough for both of us!

So we cared together for each other
>   and for our larger families.
When they came to celebrate the festivals,
>   they knew our home was always open,
>   our hearts always ready to absorb their lives.

And so it was quite a shock
>   the day that Zechariah came home

Silent.

It had been his day to burn the incense!
        The holiest of days in a priest's life!
Day after day, he would dress in his robes
        and go to the temple to wait for the day
        when the Lord would appoint him
        through the tossing of the sacred stones:
Appoint him to commune with the Lord God of Israel Himself!

And then the blessed day came...
        and Zechariah was struck dumb!
The people outside the Temple had waited and waited
        for him to show himself after the sacrifice,
        to tell if there were any word from the Lord.
But when he finally emerged,
        there was only the glow on his face,
        awe in his eyes,
        and silence on his lips,
So the people knew he had seen a vision,
        only no-one was sure what it had been!

Having a silent husband was strange indeed.
        The house seemed to echo the silence from all sides.
I found myself speaking just to remind myself
        that speech was possible!
I took to reciting the scriptures
        that Zechariah had repeated for us both
                day after day
                year after year.

One day I was reciting the story of the Maccabees,
        those fearless freedom fighters
        who had restored Jerusalem the last time.
When my lips recited the name of John,
        grandfather of the Maccabees,
John's eyes met mine with a wild determination.
No more was spoken,

only a knowledge between us
that Silence was birthing a new John.

I wasn't really surprised soon after that
When my body began to tell me
      that it wasn't Silent anymore.
Life had begun again.
There was a new hope beginning,
      a new freedom to be claimed.

My body, yes, was old for childbearing,
      but it managed.
It stretched and gurgled
      and moved and ached
      in new and amazing ways.
And Silent Zechariah
      seemed to have absorbed in his silence
A new understanding of what was needed.

I think it's fair to say
That we 'talked' more in those days
      than we had in all the years before.
Eye contact.
Smiles and frowns
      conveyed scrolls of meaning.

It was one of those silent-alive days some months later
      when my cousin Mary arrived on our threshold.
Mary was much younger,
      and I had known her all through her childhood.
Though she lived in Nazareth,
      she came with her family to Jerusalem for the festivals.

Mary was young, yes,
      but she had always been wise.
She, too, knew Silence.
Intuitively, we spent our festival times together
      in quietness,

away from the noise of the others,
cooking or cleaning,
caring for others,
sharing a silence.

When she arrived that evening,
she called out to me.
The silence of the house shattered
like a sudden clap of thunder
heralding the end of drought.

The baby within me jolted,
and I knew that moment
That the Holy One was among us.

Like the gentle rains that begin the storm,
we wept and held each other.
One glance at that dear face
now shining beneath its aura of weariness and question:
I knew at once —
the child within me knew! —
That the Holy One was among us:
God's Oath fulfilled in our midst.

In that holy moment,
My silence was completely broken
with the shouts and laughter and sobs
of the Holy Spirit.
I greeted and held this most blessed woman.
The Lord's Promise was with us,
in my very house!
Alive and well
inside the womb of my kinswoman.

And inside my womb was the messenger,
the one to tell all: the Lord is Near!

Mary stayed with me those last months.

We laughed and cried together.
We dreamed and wrestled with our fears.
We prayed and recited scripture to each other
       and even dared to sing a little.

She left shortly before my time came.
I hardly had time to mourn her leaving,
       when my womb could no longer contain
       the bundle of wild promise it held.

I called him John from the very first moment,
       even before the priests and neighbours
       came to offer blessings and prayers on the eighth day.
They thought me strange,
       bestowing such a revolutionary name
       on a baby born into quiet respectability.
They were not used to hearing my voice,
       and so they did not know how to hear it.

So they turned to Zechariah.
"His name is John," he said,
       and they all left, waggling their heads,
       not knowing whether to be amazed at the name
       or the break in Zechariah's silence.

Well, we weren't a very silent household after that.
       All three of us seemed to have found our tongues!
The walls often seemed to creak more in relief of the night—
       echoing their responses to the noisy days!

I knew my John was a holy one,
       so I taught him the holy ways of the priestly house,
       and I taught him the holy ways of the wilderness.
I knew that the holy ones
       needed to know the Silence, too.
Sometimes I would take him out to the wilderness
       where he could hear the wind
And the Ruah Spirit

       rushing through the sand and brush,
       rushing against his skin,
       pressing to enter his own breath,
Enter his own spirit,
       and unite it to the Holy One of Israel.
==

He has been gone many months now.
       He chose the desert as his temple.
       He chose the sands as his sanctuary,
       the Jordan as his pulpit.
He proclaims loudly
       what I knew most keenly
       in my Silence:

That the Holy One of Israel is near;
That we must listen with our whole bodies:
       cleanse ourselves to hear and prepare
       the Way of the Lord
          in our very midst.

MARY'S SONG
(Luke 1:26-56)

So, you've met Elizabeth, too?
        What a treasure she is!
She's the best friend — the best cousin,
A girl — a woman
        could have!

Girl? Woman?
        What am I these days?
Child of my mother?
        Mother of a child to be?
Blessed?
        Cursed?
Holy?
        Defiled?
Submissive?
        Rebellious?

Rebellious was the name my mother gave me.
Like Miriam of old,
        learning to submit to another
        has been hard work.

Submitting to the women's work
        when the outside fields and pastures

call my name so loudly:
Mary! Mary!
      Consider the lilies of the field!
      they don't sew or wash or cook!
      yet God cares for them!

Submitting to being engaged to Joseph —
      A good man, to be sure,
            but so much older.
They say I need someone older
      to teach me life.
      To teach me respectability.
         Is that life?

Anyway, he is a good man.
He has not thrown me out
      like the others would have...
He knows...

He knows, I think,
      how hard it was to submit to the angel.

It was a fearful time!
The angel said, "Peace" to me.
      He said, "Blessing."
      He said, "Don't be afraid!"
But what sense does that make?

I knew one day the Lord would bless my womb
      and I would be a mother,
But not yet!
Not now! I am still a child!
      Only engaged!
      Not yet Wife...
      Certainly not Mother
         to a King...
         to the Holy One...
How can this be?

Lord, if that is You
      in that angel disguise,
Lord, you must tell me:
      How can this be?
How can Holiness
      be born of Rebellion?
Or is Holiness
      ONLY born of Rebellion?
Rebellion against a way of living
      that is so respectable
      that it knows no Life...

How can virginity
      produce life?
Or is it that real life
      can only come from the purity
      that one has protected as one's own?

There were so many questions that day,
So many risks and challenges
      to all I knew and held dear;
So much turmoil,
      that to rebel against the confusion
      was to submit.

And so I, Mary,
      Rebellious One,
Conceived a Child
      of the most Holy One.

No longer rebellious Child,
      I was With Child.
Suddenly my body contained another
      so that I was Community with myself!

And yet, I was alone like never before.
How to explain to my mother?
      My father? Joseph? Anyone?

The Holy One led me to Elizabeth,
      Blessed Elizabeth,
God's promise to me
      that I was not alone.

Elizabeth, whose knowing eyes,
      whose hearing heart
Grasped the full impact of my condition
      in a single splendid moment,
And in doing so,
      calmed my heart,
      my fears,
      my racing pulse,
      my pounding head,
      my aching bones.

My child will know,
      her child will know,
The joy of Community,
      will they not?

Will they know as well
      the strain of community?
Will they work to rebel
      against the rich and powerful
Who grind the little ones into the earth?

Will they rebel against
      hunger and cruelty
      and sickness and despair?
Will they respect the lowly
      and remember the soil from which we all come?

Ah, Jesus,
      if I may call you that now,
Dear child inside me:
      will you know to submit

Only to the goodness of the Holy One
  who created us all?
Holy One, will you stand strong
  when they try to make you respectable?

"My heart praises the Lord!
My soul, my spirit within me, is glad
  because of God my Saviour.
For he has remembered,
He has heard me, his lowly rebellious servant!
From now on, all people will call me blessed
  because of the great things
  the Mighty God has done for me.

"His name is Holy from one generation to another.
  He shows mercy to those who honour him.

"He has stretched out his mighty arm
  and scattered the proud
  In the imaginations of their hearts.

"He has brought down mighty kings from their thrones
  and lifted up the lowly.

"He has filled the hungry with good things
  and sent the rich away with empty hands.

"He has kept the promise he made to our ancestors
  and has come to the help of his rebellious servant Israel.

"He has remembered to show mercy to Abraham
  and to all his descendants forever!

"Blessed be the Lord God of Israel
  who has blessed his rebellious servant
   and given us New Life."

Blessed be the One who has not left me alone.

ANNA'S SONG
(Luke 2:21-38)

Come! Come sit beside me and hear my song!
        I have seen the Promised One!
Mine eyes have seen the coming of the Lord!
In this very place,
        this holy temple
        this house of the Most Holy God of Israel:
I have seen the Promised One!

Ah! It's good of you to come and sit with this old woman.
        So many just shake their heads and keep on walking.
They see my shriveled limbs
        and think my brain has shriveled as well.
They hurry to get out of my way,
        as if I will pass 'old age' on to them!

How little they know of what I have to pass on.
I've sat here in the Women's Court
        these scores of years
Since my husband died,
        since my daughters left home...
I had nothing to keep them back,
        and there was nothing to keep me there,
So I came here.
A good life it's been,

though so few recognise the goodness...
They're so busy running around,
      caring for the world,
            but not caring for their souls,
Their souls that cry out for rest
      for nourishment
      for peace.

That's what I find here: Peace.
I look around at these stone walls and pillars,
      at the altars and the temple courts.
I never tire of the rhythm,
      the prayers,
      the readings,
      the scriptures,
      the songs,
      the festivals.

Why do the others want to pass by so quickly?
Why not sit in the Presence,
      in the house of the Lord?

Sometimes I listen to the squeals of the young goats
      being slaughtered for sacrifice.
I hear the doves cooing
      till their blood gurgles out
            as an offering to the Lord.
Offering their life blood for something greater...

Sometimes I just sit and watch the people
      coming and going.
Everyone wants to come to Jerusalem,
      to the temple.
But as soon as they're here,
      they're ready to leave again!
What is it that pulls them on?
What gives them so little time
      to rest in the Lord?

They say I'm too old to remember!
      Maybe so, maybe so.
I remember my babies:
        awake all night it seemed
        till I could fall asleep standing up!
But that was only for a season,
        and even then I was blessed, so blessed...

I remember tending the house,
        tending the children,
        tending the crops,
        waiting for the harvest...
Sometimes it came.
        Sometimes it didn't.

I remember the years of waiting for the Promised One,
        of listening to the scriptures,
        praying, fasting,
Waiting for the One who would deliver Israel from its woes:
        Yahweh will never leave his people alone for long!
Yahweh is patient and compassionate,
        even when we are breathless and in a hurry.

And now,
Yes, I've told you already!
        I've seen the Promised One!
With these old and feeble eyes,
        I have seen the Glory of the Lord!

Old Simeon saw him first.
The young couple had come all the way from Bethlehem.
They didn't need to come...
        They could have offered the sacrifices there.
It was plain from their dress,
        their sacrifices,
That they didn't need the extra expense
        of coming to Jerusalem with the child.

But they came,
>as if they knew they were about
>>Holy Business.
It was her face I saw first –
>wise beyond her years.
Yet childlike in expectation
>as she handed the child to Simeon.

I saw him lift the child to the heavens,
And I knew... I knew then...
>that I had seen the Promised One
>>who will lead his people ... into peace.

When they had finished their sacrifice,
>they began walking in the direction of the Women's Court.
I realized they were walking directly toward me,
>and I was trembling!

Did they know I'd been watching them?
>Could they hear the pounding of my poor frail heart?
>Could they see the tears in my eyes,
>>the quivering of my bones?

The young woman's eyes were calm,
>yet they glinted with quiet excitement.
I think she, too, was quivering inside,
>because she bit on her bottom lip
>>as she handed the child to me.

I willed my bones to stop their shaking,
>as I held the child to the heavens.
Most Blessed Yahweh!
>I have seen with my own eyes
>your Anointed One!
>The Long-expected One
>come to set your people free!
Thank you, thank you,

Thank you, Lord God King of the Universe!

I guess I must have been quivering a little too much,
  for the young father took the child from me after that,
His strong arms a much better protection
  than my trembling limbs...

But I have seen the Lord!
  I've been telling whoever would listen all day long.
They smile at me and hurry away,
  their faces trying to conceal their amusement –
At this old woman and her wild imagination...
  but have they taken the time to watch and wait
    and look for God's presence themselves?

I'm glad you've sat with me for a while
  and listened to my old woman's story.
Now that I've seen the Lord's Promised One,
  I don't think Yahweh will keep me here much longer.
My days in this temple are coming to an end...

And I know you must be going now, too,
  off to your children and crops and chores.
But you'll tell them, won't you?
You'll tell the people that
  the Promised One has come
    to save Israel,
    to save us?

Tell them, if you must,
that you only have the word
  of the old woman, Anna,
  The Favoured One.
But tell them!
  Tell them the Lord has come amongst us!

THE BEATEN BATH:
A WOMAN IN THE TIME OF JOHN THE BAPTIST
(Luke 3:1-20)

What? You're still here?
Not running off to the desert
      like the rest of them?
They've all gone:
      the old ones, the young ones,
      the men,
      the children following along,
Even the women!

Well, you won't find this old woman
      running off to the wilderness
      to see that crazy man,
Especially with all the work to be done!
      Floors to clean!
      Bread to bake!
Even my daughters-in-law have run off,
      left all the work to me!

And it's the DESERT they run to!
The sheep run off to the desert
      to get themselves lost!
And the desert is where the demons stay!
      Devils!
      Wild animals!

No roof to shade from the scorching sun,
        no walls to keep out the frozen starry sky.
Grown men lose their senses
        out in the desert.
Only the prophets can survive that madness,
        but Elijah is long gone,
        and it's been so long since another's come...

Of course, they say this new one
        is Elijah come again.
This one, John, I think they call him,
        wears 'prophet clothes'
        and eats 'prophet food.'
But he says such strange things!
He acts like we Jews are the ones
        who have to change,
        Like we're the ones causing all the problems.
Hasn't he seen what the Romans are doing to us?
After all we've been through,
        he says, "WE have to change:
"Make the path straight," he says!

Well, I'll tell you this:
The path is there because that's the easiest way to get around.
        and it's well-worn because it works.
The well-worn path
        is the one that keeps us going
        from here to there
        without going crazy in this madness.

Everybody knows the path.
Even the cows and the sheep follow it:
Just follow the beaten path.
Who has time to straighten it out?
There are floors to sweep,
        food to cook,
        dishes to scrub,
        clothes to wash,

clothes to mend….

Of course, if you're just going to eat
        locusts and wild honey,
Then I guess there's plenty of time
        for straightening out paths,
But this family likes a little barley and olive oil,
        goat's milk and cheese;
And that means the goats have to be milked,
        and the cheese has to be made by SOMEONE,
And this family wants their floors swept
        and their sleeping mats straightened out,
        and somebody's got to do it!
So, I tell you:
If all the work is going to get done,
        if you're going to get from here to there,
You use the beaten path.
        the old ways are best.

But what do the young ones know?
Some new guy goes out to the wilderness
        and starts saying crazy things,
        and they all run out to see,
Well, let them go:
Go jump in the water
        and get baptised by this crazy guy!

Now THERE's a crazy idea: BAPTISED!
Just like they were some gentile heathens
        trying to become one of us.
FOREIGNERS they are, stealing all the ripe figs off the trees,
        all the sweet ripe girls from the good families –
GENTILES they are,
        whose ancestors never wandered through the wilderness—
God gave US the land.

These others come and try to become Jews
        by being baptised!

And then this guy says
>we JEWS have to be baptised!
As if we weren't already God's chosen ones...

Now they tell me everyone is down there by the Jordan
>confessing their sins to everyone.
Well, my Zanaiah did all the confessions for this family
>when he was alive,
>and now my sons do it,
But they've always done it privately
>when they went to the Temple.
None of this public spewing out of Family Matters.
This is a respectable family,
>and we've kept ourselves
>respectable.

Now I hear that even some of the WOMEN
>are going down to be baptised!
With all those folks around!
Confessing in public!
It's too much for an old woman like me.
Give me beaten paths.
Give me respectability.
Give me floors to sweep...

Clean floors –
Yes, my daughters-in-law did seem to remember
>him saying something about clean floors,
Though little they would know
>about cleaning floors themselves!
This John fellow was talking about
>one who was coming after him—
That he would be cleaning the floors
>of the threshing hall,
>storing the grain,
>sweeping out the chaff.
Well, if the one who's coming
>knows about clean floors,

Then I like that!

Throw out the chaff!
The foreigners,
Those horrible Romans and Gentiles!
Throw them all out, Yahweh!
We're your people, Yahweh!
Turn them out so we can live respectable lives!

Ha! I'd like to have been there
      when those Pharisees and Sadducees
      came to see that John guy.
They say he called them, 'Sons of Snakes.'
Ha! That's a good one!
I can just see them crawling along
      on their bellies in the dust!
All those rules they follow
      and try to make US follow —
More and more rules
      of THEIR Kind of respectability
      trying to make us ashamed of ourselves.
A clean floor: that's respectability!

My sons say John told the Pharisees
      that they had to do the things
      that showed they had turned back to God.
Maybe the Pharisees don't know
      that God likes clean floors,
      so they keep making up new rules.

But then I heard my sons saying
      that John had told them that if they didn't change,
God would raise up children of Abraham
      from the stones!
Have you ever heard anything so crazy?
Most of the children of Abraham have been 'raised up'
      from nights spent on stone floors anyway,
But it still takes good Jewish Seed

to raise up children of Abraham!

The other part I didn't understand
       was about the axe being ready
       to cut down trees that don't bear good fruit—
Well, that makes sense,
       if he's talking about all the bad seeds coming
How can bad seed bear good fruit?
But they seem to think
       he means we Jews are subject
       to this same axe!

Well, I've borne good fruit:
       six sons
       three daughters;
Buried five of them
       along with my Zanaiah,
But I've done my part, God!
I've lit the Sabbath candles
       and kept the fires burning.
I've kept this house clean
       through dust storms and muddy feet,
       goats and disease,
       through the hardships
          of Romans and foreigners,
       through my mother-in-law
          and daughters-in-law,
       through children and grandchildren:
I've kept it clean!

And now they all leave me alone
       to run out to the desert after this fool.
But I've kept this house clean, Lord!
I've followed the beaten path.
I've born good fruit!
Will you cut me down, too?
==
What I really can't understand,

is why they all come back looking so happy every day.
They're just bubbling full of noise and laughter!
They come back dancing,
        dusty feet all over the clean floors!
Can't stop babbling
        about how they feel so relieved from their burden —
So they make more burdens for me!
Was there ever a time
        when there weren't burdens for me?
How can they be so happy?
How can they keep...
        singing?
They say he talks about the axe chopping things down
        and judgment
        and burning in fire,
But they come back happy!
So full of life!

They talk about the Promised One coming,
        as if after waiting for 4000 years,
        they think he's coming HERE and NOW!
Well, if he comes here,
        this will be the only clean house in the village.
My house is clean.

One problem with a clean house is...
It's so.... quiet.
It's so quiet
        when they've all gone away.
I almost miss the babbling.
I wonder...
        do they miss this nagging old woman?
Maybe they're glad to be rid of me for a while.
But someone's got to keep the fire burning
        and those floors clean
        And the path beaten;
Someone's got to keep the family respectable!
We can't all go running off

to see the crazy man in the desert.
==
My house is clean.
     and now there's the marketing to do ...
The market's on the beaten path and...
     the desert is just a few steps further.
Maybe there's time to go see
     what all the fuss is about
It's just a few steps from the beaten path....

MARY AT CANA
(John 2:1-11)

It's hard to see him go.
      It's hard to see any of your children go—
Even when they're grown –
      thirty years old he is now!
They leave many times, it seems.
Still, each time they step out of the door
      they take with them another piece of your heart.

You know they have to go:
      fulfil all they were meant to be,
All you raised them to be,
      all God intended them to be!
And yet the whole world seems a little emptier,
      a little darker and lonelier,
Each time your grown child steps
      from the inside womb of your home
      into the quivering void of the unknown.

We've had a good time these past few days on holiday together,
      coming down from the hills of Galilee
            to rest after the busy-ness of the wedding at Cana,
      coming down to Capernaum, where the city meets the sea.
The city, with its hustle and bustle and endless agenda;
The sea, with its mystery and madness,
      one moment angry and threatening,

92

the next moment still as silence.

The sea always fascinates me.
We know how to do the rhythms of the city
        because we control them to some extent
But the sea is ever a challenge —
        like the future —
As we test our skills against a force larger than ourselves,
        as we steer our craft against the elements.

The best prepared are those who have trained enough
        to know their craft
But not too much to fall complacent in what they know
        and so misjudge the elements...

That's the job we mothers do: we train our children –
        from the moment our child breathes
                its first gasping, squalling breath
        till the day we finally nudge them
                out and over our doorstep:
We prepare them for their part in the world.
We watch their every movement,
        scan the horizons of their souls and bodies constantly
                for hints of secret treasures
                the Lord has lain within their soul:
        Rough unpolished gems,
                or scraggly, unpruned shoots needing a firm hand:
What talents, what gifts, what mysteries
        has the Lord planted in them
        that will be needed — urgently needed! –
        for the world to survive?
We watch them intently with one eye –
        while the other is firmly set on the world around them.
What traps lie waiting in their path?
        What snares to trip them up?
What needs are crying out that our child must hear and answer?

It is a consuming job, this job of watching and waiting,

planting and pruning,
weighing the balances,
measuring the readiness
           and the spirit and the understanding.
We do it.
We do it with love, fierce love,
      with a determination:
This child that God has entrusted to our care
      will be ready when the time comes...

With Jesus, my eldest, it often seemed my job consisted
            of running to keep up with him!
So full of energy, of love and creativity he was!
            So full of understanding and care as well...
So often it was I who would stumble
            trying to explain something to him —
Like the way the Lord made the rain come in its time
            to turn the earth to bounty;
            the heaven-sent water sprouting
                  into the honeyed juice of the grape
Or the desert turning into palatial splendour
            or the birds learning to trust their wings to the wind.
He would listen quietly to my feeble groping at these miracles,
He would nod like an old man,
            as if he'd always known that
            and was a little surprised
            that I found it necessary to explain it to him.

But I wanted him to see!
            and I wanted to see for myself,
And so often I saw it all the clearer
            for having pointed it out to him.

More than any other of my children,
            he seemed to know these things
But often I wondered if he knew things about himself –
            if he could see how perfectly his talent
            measured up with the needs all around...

Could he see how thirsty the people were
    to drink of the trust and honesty
    that flowed from his very being?

John had seen it – my nephew John, his cousin,
    just a few months older than he —
John, too, had a holiness about him
    That the world responded to
        with open-mouthed eagerness.

The day I heard John speak of him as 'The Lamb of God,'
    my heart jumped — as Elizabeth said hers did
    when she first met me pregnant with Jesus.
Whoever had heard of a person described as 'the Lamb of God'?
    And yet it fit.
It fit and it hurt,
    for sacrificial lamb is of course meant to be sacrificed.
A beautiful offering, yes,
    but could it not be someone else's son to bear that name?

It fit – and it hurt – in ways that I could only begin to grasp.
Like the grape, when it is only a tiny hard bud,
    before it is full and ripe and ready,
    there is a truth in it of what is to come.
When John said it, my heart jumped,
    and I gasped for a moment —
For I could sense the time of ripening was coming near.

And then others began to note the secret unfolding within him.
Some of his brothers suddenly looking at him
    with slightly different eyes.
The sometimes-awkward strangeness of his boyhood
    Somehow seeming now to make more sense.

A few others, 'disciples,' they called themselves –
    caught a glimpse of What Could Be –
Not just in him
    but in what they themselves became with him –

They began to call him 'Rabbi' and 'Son of God,'
    as people do when they meet someone
    whose identity is more than meets the eye.
Some called him 'the one Moses and the prophets spoke about'
    and one dubbed him 'King of Israel.'
Others dared to breathe the word 'Messiah.'

Each time I caught my breath.
    Each time I glanced at his face to see if he had heard.
Each time, the look came back,
The look from his childhood,
    patiently 'knowing,'
    impatiently wondering why it made such a difference
        to all the rest of us.

And then we were all at the wedding.
    with the cheerful chatter and the giddy excitement.
Jesus was always good at parties –
    he knew how to celebrate like no other!
Just having him there always made the festivities more festive.

And then there was that lull,
    the gradually growing silence
    when no one is quite sure
        where the party spirit has gone.
At home, we would say, "the wine has run out" —
    and we would know that it's either time
        to send everybody home
        and hope they won't quite remember tomorrow
        that our party ended too early –
Or it's time to get the party restarted on a different level...

At home, Jesus had only to hear 'the wine has run out'
    and he would start telling a new story,
    or he would get that twinkle in his eye,
And before you knew it,
    we'd all be laughing and celebrating again!
I never knew exactly what he'd do,

Only that he would find some new and creative way
        to make the Spirit flow again...

When the lull came this time, the room was full of people,
        and he was sitting there
                with his brothers and disciples all around –
Anyone would think he was the host instead of the guest
        the way people were hanging on his every word.

From my position a little distance away
        I could see he was holding back today.
Even with half the town eager to be close to him,
        he wasn't giving it his all.
My mother-eye saw his knuckles
        holding his cloak a little too tightly,
As if he weren't yet ready to let go
        and be his true self with all these others around.

The pounding that started in my head
        told me his time was near –
        very near.
The time for which we, he and I –
        and his father when he was with us —
Had prepared these many years.
The lamb being led to a new pasture,
        the grape ready to be plucked.

I wanted to tell him, 'the wine has run out'
        but that wasn't all of it.
I wanted him to know as well
        that he had what they all were craving...
And so, I made my way across the room
And found the words changing themselves in the process:
        '*They* have no wine,' I whispered in his ear.

At first, he seemed annoyed.
Not just with me,
        but perhaps with my confirmation

of what he had recognised on his own:
His time had come —
  the time to step out of the old wine skin
  and into the new adventure.

As I watched the struggle on his face,
  I knew him being born in a new way.
As his knuckles relaxed against his cloak,
  I whispered to the servant to do whatever he told them.

The rest of course, has been all the talk of the past few days.
Everyone amazed to taste the new wine
  where before there had only been water.
Everyone seemingly forgetting that the Lord our God
   does that miracle every day all around us:
   The gifts of the heavens
     turning into the fullness of the vine around us.
Everyone incredulous that the last wine
  should be better than the first,
So steeped were they in looking backward for the Holy
   instead of looking to the future
   or even grasping the present moment.

In those moments I saw for myself
  what I had always imagined would be beyond my sphere:
That the Present Moment far exceeded
  the glories of the preparation times.

I thought I had let him go so many times before,
   but this time I sensed my job had been done,
   at least the part that was mine alone to do.
He now belonged to another realm,
   taking into the public space
   the holiness of new wine.
Becoming celebration for all to enter,
  all those who dared to drink the cup.

A part of myself was torn from me

but also torn of my own volition –
For how could I keep to myself
      what the whole world needed?

And now he has left once again,
      and the house is silent.
And yet, as I walk back through the rooms,
      his Spirit is with me still.
As if my preparing for him to be what he was meant to be
      was also preparing myself to fully receive
      all he could be for me.

I see he has left me some wine:
      enough to sip and savour,
      enough to warn and welcome me
      enough to remind me
          that his Spirit will never fully leave me.
Amen.

SIMON'S MOTHER-IN-LAW
(Mark 1:29-39)

My life was one of early mornings!
The men leaving early before the sky was beginning to colour...
     I was up with them to stir the ashes and revive the fire
     and see them off.
Even when my bones got old
     and longed to stay on the sleeping mat,
The men were going off, so I was up as well...

The men were off to serve the sea another day –
Setting their muscles and wits
     against the waves and the sun,
Setting their strength and stamina and nets
     towards the fishes beneath the waters.
I was up to serve the needs of the household...

I had served my father's household first,
     then my husband's,
     and now my daughter's husband, Simon,
        who took me in when I became a widow.
I would stoke the fire and make the breakfast.
My daughter would prod the children from their mats
     and set them at their chores.
Sometimes I would stand at the door and strain my eyes
     to search the last pinpoint of the boat on the horizon.
Each day I would watch and wonder –

would the men return that evening,
Boat full of fish? Mouths full of stories?
Singing the song of the sea and the sky?
       Feast or fast?
       Full – or empty and dejected?
Would Simon and the others disappear from us
       as my husband had:
       swallowed up by the sea he served?

Most days there was little time to stand and watch the sea...
Instead there was the rhythm of our days:
       cooking, cleaning, minding the children,
       preparing the previous day's catch,
       readying it for the market.
       mending the nets...
Always one eye out on the horizon.
       waiting for the boats to bring our menfolk back...
Then spread out the nets again,
       sort and clean and salt the fish,
       serve the sea that in turn served us all.
==
We heard about The Stranger first at the market –
       the news coming fresh from the synagogue.
He had preached there,
       and the people said he was different:
       a God-man in our midst!
It was all a little exciting –
       and a little fearful –
How to know if he were for real?

Simon seemed particularly taken with the news of the Stranger.
A raw, strapping fellow Our Simon was:
       quick with his nets,
       quick with his mouth
       quick to act or speak
          and then to think later –
But he had a good heart inside of him:
       an honest bloke if ever there was one.

Each evening Simon asked of the news from the market:
      Had anyone seen The Stranger recently?
      What news from the synagogue?
      Was this the One who would save us from the Romans?
      Was this One ready for the fight?

Simon had been ready to go to the Jordan himself
      where we'd heard that Jesus
            had been with John the Baptist.
Simon said he just wanted to take a look...
      but we had persuaded him not to go just yet –
And then this Jesus fellow had disappeared for a while,
      into the wilderness, some said –
Which was enough to convince me
      that this was NOT what we needed.
The wilderness is no place for family men,
      certainly no place for fishermen!
      especially fishermen with families to support...
Sure, there was still Andrew to help the family out,
      but Andrew was starting to get interested
            in the Jesus stories as well...
What would happen to us if they both....?
      Well, it was too much to think about.

Then there was the evening when they didn't come home.
We scanned the horizon for their boats
      in the fast-fading light –
Some evenings it took longer to get the catch in.
      Sometimes they stayed out all night.
But this evening the stories started coming back
      about how they'd left their boats... their nets...
            left it all behind!
For what? Some said it was The Stranger...

It was quiet in the house that evening.
      Too quiet.
No one could put words around our feelings:

confused
abandoned
slow building anger
frustrated helplessness...
We fed the children and put them to bed.
We scrubbed the pots
      and re-salted the previous day's fish
      and counted the sacks of meal in the cupboard
      and peered at the oil left in the jars.
We swept the hearth
      and chased out the cats
      and scrubbed down the table.
Scrubbed the floor.
      Scrubbed the table again.
Then sat down to wait.

And wait.
An empty sort of waiting, not knowing what was next.
Would they come back?
Surely they would!
      Fishing was their life!
      Sea water was in their blood!
What does a fisher do in the morning
      if not set out in a boat?

It was as if I were suddenly widowed again –
And yet we heard reports that they were still alive –
      so very much alive!

Could they think so little of us
      that they would leave us behind?
Did our service mean so little?
Did our survival mean so little?
      How would we eat?
      How would we sleep?

The hired men still went out –
      they still brought us some fish to sort and clean,

But it wasn't the same –
and who knew how long the hired ones would stay around?

It was the worry that finally got me down.
We'd been determined to keep the family going –
the floors clean and the bread made
and the fish salted,
But we found ourselves staring back at the fish
with eyes as dead as their own
and bodies just as lifeless....
==
I hardly noticed the difference
when they said I had the fever.
My head had been going in circles for days.
One morning I could think of no reason to get up –
no fire to start or boat to push off the shore.
No reason to leave my mat.

My daughter had called and called –
claiming there was still work to do...
Then she laid her cold hand on my head
and hissed to the others:
"Go and get the doctor!"

The scurry of feet, the whispering in the corner...
A new quiet, too quiet, descending,
so quiet it woke me from my fevered sleep.

They'd all gone!
Only me left –
They've all gone after The Stranger!
and left me to die here on my own.
A woman without her brood
can live no longer than a fish without the sea.
No one to serve,
no one to scold,
no one to hold,
No one... no one...

I slept again,
>	and fell down, down into the nets of the sea.
Strangling … black darkness…
>	Biting cold… scalding heat.

Then voices returning
>	and feet pounding…
Women's voices, men's voices… urgent.
In my hazy underwater,
>	the voice of my husband,
>	my son-in-law…
>	Simon was always louder than the rest!

And then another hand on my head,
Not cold like my daughter's
>	but warm and calm and powerful,
Heavier than a woman's hand,
>	strong… yet gentle.
The hand was taking mine
>	and lifting me up
pulling me from the depths of the water
>	out of the choking darkness
>	up from the tangling nets,
>	up from the pits of despair….
>	up into the light of day,
The air suddenly warm and full –
>	full of people and faces
>	eyes intent on me…
Calling me from my depths…
Hand full of power and purpose
>	lifting me up,
>	lifting me up.

Then I was standing, feeling so full of life
>	that I felt like dancing,
Like it was my wedding day all over again!
>	with tambourines and drums – let's dance!

So many people ... in my house...
They must be hungry ... and thirsty...
I can feed them!
>There's still some bread and some salted fish...
>There are still a few figs and some goat's milk.
Let's feast!
Let me serve you!

That's when I realised: The Stranger was the one in my house –
>filling it full to overflowing –
The universe, the earth, the skies,
>all dancing within the space of my house!

Jesus' hand had come to me
>not to take it all away
>not to steal all my life contained
>not to leave me empty and lifeless
But to return to me my purpose
>to remind me how to serve again.

I got right to those pots,
>stirred up the fire,
>filled the kettle on the hearth –
There was work to do!
>and everyone was laughing and singing
>and shouting the news.
Soon all the neighbours had come,
>Singing and dancing and bringing along still others,
>falling over each other in our joy.

For Jesus had come to our house,
and Jesus had reminded us that it is in our serving that we are most alive!
Thank you, Jesus,
>for coming to our house
>and taking my son-in-law
>and giving us back our lives, our love,
>our purpose: our service.

LOVING LIKE A MOTHER
(Mark 10:2-16)

Ah! It's been a long day – but it's been a good day.
        Actually, it's been a GREAT day!
Come to think of it,
        it's probably been one of the best days of my life!
It's not every day that you come face to face
        with the answers to everything you've ever asked…
It's not every day that you meet the One
        you've been waiting for all your life…
The One that everyone's been waiting for –
        for ever and ever and ever….

Started out early this morning.
Actually, I guess it started out a few days ago
        when we first heard that he was coming to our town…
The stories had long preceded him –
        this Jesus of Nazareth –
Some of the stories were quite unbelievable –
How he'd healed people – men, women, even children —
        people with horrendous demons
        people that no one else would even touch!
Well, this Jesus didn't seem to care about those 'rules'
The way I heard it,
        Jesus was just there for whoever needed him –
        healing and talking and just being with people
        in the way they needed it most.

I liked that.

They said he was a good preacher, too,
But preachers come and go,
        some of them are loud
        and some of them know all the fancy words
But when their breath is gone,
        the words are gone, too.
What stays on is what they've done
        and how they've done it.

The stories I'd heard about Jesus
        told me that he really cared about people –
Especially the little ones
        that others seemed to disregard.
I like that.
It's what I'd always imagined –
        Well, at least, HOPED –
        that God was like.
Not so big and powerful
        that he couldn't remember the little people.

My kids had heard the stories, too.
        Kids know good stories when they hear them.
They listened carefully when their father told them
        what he'd heard in the marketplace.
But they'd heard the stories themselves, too,
        playing in the streets.

When I tucked them into bed at night,
        and kissed them good night,
They'd whisper the stories to me
        with the unspoken question hanging in their voices,
"Is Jesus really that good?"
        Or was it just another wistful whim
                of our Hebrew wanderings?
Was God really coming to us?

As I blew out the candle near their sleeping mats,
      I would wonder myself: Is God really here among us?
Sometimes my heart would pound so hard at the thought,
      that I could scarcely breathe.
I certainly couldn't give them a full answer myself.
"Wait and see," was the best I could muster.
We Hebrews are good at waiting.
      Seeing would be the test.

When we heard last evening
      that he would be in our village this morning,
We could hardly sleep.
It was well after the stars were beginning to fade
      and elusive sleep was no longer to be chased after
That I made up my mind.
We WOULD go and see.

As soon as my husband was out of the house,
      I had the children up
      and urged them on to get their chores finished quickly!
We race through milking the goat and sweeping the floor
      and washing up...
Jesus was just nearby
      and we had to go see for ourselves!

If the truth be told,
I wanted a little more than just seeing.
Especially for the children.
I wanted the touch.
      that would be the real test for me.
So many of the rules were about forbidding touch.
      Men not touching women.
      No one – at least no one respectable — touching blood.
      No one touching illness.
      No one touching death.
Even when my children were born,
      the taboos were there.
I wanted to hold the babies tight

and trace the incredible shapes of their noses and ears
and fingers and toes...
Even the warm and shiny ooze of blood and water
that bathed them when they were first born
seemed magical to me –
But they were soon whisked away to be cleaned
and swaddled, wrapped up tight...
As soon as the midwife left,
I gathered them back again.
Close to me.
Close enough to touch and feel their breath,
their spirit with me.
They who had come so recently from heaven
seemed to have the brush of heaven
Still on their skin and breath...
What I'd heard of Jesus made me think
that he might know something of that too –
the freshness of heaven in our midst.

I wanted the touch to happen.
I wanted Jesus to touch my children.
and I wanted my children to touch Jesus.
I had the feeling – the certainty –
That if they could touch,
we might all be reconnected with heaven again.

Is that too much to ask?

I certainly didn't tell anyone else about my plan –
But as soon as we had rushed through the chores
and were out on the street,
I realized that everyone else seemed to have the same idea!
There was Miriam and Ruth and Judith –
all hurrying out with their own children in tow –
Rushing towards the same place –
the place where we'd heard Jesus was to be...

We were all breathless by the time we got there,

the children wide-eyed
>and dancing from foot to foot in excitement...
The mothers trying hard to
>keep scarves and robes and shawls in proper places,
With an eye out as well
>for the best place to stand in the crowd...

And then we saw him – just up above –
But wouldn't you know?
>the Pharisees had got there first!
And, just as we'd heard from other places,
They were pestering him with all their fancy questions –
>in their oh-so-proper voices
>with their oh-so-proper questions
>about their oh-so-proper rules!

It was enough to make me scream.
I looked sideways
>to see my neighbour Ruth biting her tongue as well...
They were going on about divorce –
Ah! Couldn't they just leave things alone!
Everyone knew a man could divorce a woman
>any time he wanted –
>especially if he saw somebody else he liked better –
He just had to write out the paper and send her off –
It happened just last month at the other end of the village –
>I don't know the woman well,
>but I'd heard the stories and the shame
>as she covered her face and left with her children
>>to go back to her father's house.

If could happen to any of us.
We knew it.
We all cleaned and polished and cooked and sewed
>and kept the children quiet
>and bedded our husbands regularly.
But it could happen to any of us at any time –
>and we didn't want to have given any excuse for the divorce...

We watched Jesus closely to see how he would answer –
        his face seemed calm enough, but his eyes were angry.
He asked them what Moses had said –
        that was a bit of a cheeky insult, really! –
He, asking the Pharisees if they knew the Law!
        of course, they knew it...
        Every dot of it.
What Jesus seemed to be probing was:
        did they know the reason behind it?
        What the Law was really about?

My mind raced back to last Sabbath at the synagogue –
        How the elderly matriarch had raised her eyebrows
             and sniffed in our direction
        when my tiny Isaac squirmed too much during the prayers...
I held him closer and tried to concentrate his abundant energy
        into my own prayers –
Surely this one who had come so recently from God
        had much of God's energy to share with me.
It was a pity that the Matriarch wanted only
        to subdue that spirit
        instead of sharing it...
But then there are the rules!
        and squirming in synagogue is definitely against the rules!
Rules and Laws and traditions –
        in their best sense they helped us keep order in our lives
But in their worst, they squeezed the love out of our lives...

One of the children tugged on my hand then
        and brought me back to what Jesus was saying...
That God had brought man and woman together for unity
        and no one was to tear that union apart...
Yes, he was right –
        man and woman together for unity –
        to work for common unity – for community —
In that sense, the divorce question seemed ludicrous,
        crass.

The Pharisees began to quietly slip away...

And the children were tugging to go on ahead!
      "Let's go see Jesus!"
Ah, yes, we're here to see and to hear and to touch!
We wives and mothers clutched our scarves and shawls
      and allowed the children to pull us on ahead.

Until we were stopped.
I hadn't thought it of Jesus' "disciples," as they were called –
      the group that followed him around –
I had thought they would have absorbed
      some of his generous spirit
But there they were, blocking the way
      keeping the children away from Jesus –
The scowl on one of their faces looked just like the matriarch.
And then that scowl turned to bewilderment
      as Jesus saw what was happening
      and called the children to him...
And they ran and jumped and squealed with delight!
Jesus' arms opened wide and folded around so many
      that they nearly knocked him down!
I don't think he would have minded.

Sometimes love just does that:
Knocks you down to the place where you can really feel it –
      to the place where you can love
      and be loved in all its abundance.

And then he was picking up the smallest one,
      my Isaac,
      whose little legs had made him the last to get to Jesus.
And Jesus was holding him close
      and saying a blessing over him
      and all the children...
And telling everybody that God's love was like that –
      and that we had to be like a child to really love in God's way!

Well, the Pharisees had ALL slipped away by then...
        too embarrassed to be seen in public
        with a grown man holding children in his arms!

For a brief moment, I felt sorry for them –
        The Pharisees who worked so hard
                at keeping the Law and the traditions
        had completely missed the Love.
I saw Jesus looking after them with a look of sad longing,
        as if he really wanted them to understand...

And then I was going up to Jesus
        and trying to retrieve Isaac from his arms –
But, of course, Isaac didn't want to go anywhere!
        and he snuggled up closer with his arms around Jesus' neck.

Jesus smiled in my direction and whispered in Isaac's ear –
        "Your mother needs some love as well"
And soon little Isaac's arms were stretched out to me...
        to enfold me in Jesus' love, too...

My heart was ready to explode then –
        with love for Isaac, for Jesus –
        for all God's creatures!
The children and I danced all the way home.
I nearly lost my scarf several times...
We sang and laughed so much
        that more than one solemn home body
        stopped her sweeping
        long enough to stare at us...
But we didn't mind!
When you've seen what heaven's like
        respectability loses its appeal.

It was hard to put Isaac down to sleep...
        I just wanted to keep holding him forever.
The innocence of hope, the touch of love, the joy of heaven
        all wrapped up in that little bundle blessed by Jesus...

Finally he slipped off to his dreamland
      releasing me to my rest as well –
But still the aroma of love lingered on…
Ah, yes, it's been a wonderful day…

MARY'S JOURNEY
(Mark 11:1-19)

It's been a long day.
A long day – but a good day:
The streets full of people and animals,
      branches and cloaks,
      donkeys and dogs;
The air full of cheers and shouts and laughter.
      A good day.

They loved you, Jesus,
The crowds loved you today,
      as I have loved you all these years
Since we first began to journey together,
      you and me and Joseph
          all those years ago...

Another donkey carried us then —
      you and me, you still inside of me –
Another donkey carried us on that risky journey.
Hope led us on,
      even when fear threatened to intervene

Hope carried us to Bethlehem
      and then to Egypt.
Hope brought us back to the land of Judah
      and on to Galilee.

Hope took us to Nazareth
      and then to Jerusalem when you were twelve.
Do you remember those journeys, Jesus?
Those travels when Hope held our hands and carried us on?

I remember when you would get weary as a child
      and would finally ask your father to carry you home...

Home.
Home.
It would be good to go home now.
It's been a long day.
A good day.
And home would be a good place to rest.
Are you ready to go home now, Jesus?

I know what you'll answer me:
      "Home is where my Father is."
And you'll open your arms wide
      and gesture at the achingly open spaces
Where all God's children —
      all those numberless ones
      you call your sisters and brothers —
Where all Gods' children find a place.
Where all God's children find a place.

You'll open your arms wide to Jerusalem:
      the House of Shalom.
      the House of Peace.
Even as Jerusalem has opened its arms to you today, Jesus

I saw you wanting to embrace Jerusalem today, Jesus.
I saw in your eyes how you wanted Jerusalem to embrace
      Peace.
      Shalom.
But as I followed your eyes,
I could also see all the places
      where peace is still a stranger.

As I watched you in the temple this evening,
    I could see that Peace was a stranger there in the temple,
The place where Hope would pitch her tent
    especially amongst the poor...
But Peace was a stranger there,
    I could these that in your eyes.
Peace will always be a stranger
    when money is changing hand
    while Justice is ignored.

How can Jerusalem be a House of Peace
    when is Justice ignored?

I saw you in the temple today, Jesus.
    saw the familiar set of your jaw
    and squaring of your shoulders,
Even as the sadness filled your eyes,
    sadness and pity that grows into anger.

My mind races back to other journeys:
    to Cana and Capernaum.
    to Bethsaida and Bethany.
    to Tiberias and Mt Tabor.
Some journeys you let me travel with you.
    Some journey I could only follow in my heart.

Somehow we always knew the road
    would finally lead towards Jerusalem.

But the journey isn't ending there,
    is it, Jesus?

Oh Jesus, the journey's just begun, hasn't it?
    The cheers of the crowd weren't the goal, were they, Jesus?
I see it now: this is just one more stop on the road...

Where will it end?

Where will your angry compassion lead you?
I fear for you, Jesus.
If you do anymore,
      they'll kill you.
The crowd that cheered you on today
      will kill you tomorrow.
You know it, Jesus.
I know it, Jesus.
The road ahead is marked with danger.

But then, I hear you say:
Our roads have always been full of danger.
From the very first day.
      but our roads have been full of hope as well...
And Jerusalem was just another stop on the road...
And I know, my son, you won't finally stop
      until you've done your all;
      until you've given your all.
For the Shalom of Jerusalem.
      The shalom of us all.

How far is there still to travel, Jesus?
To hell and back?
Will you stop only in death?

I'm coming with you, Jesus.
I'm coming with you.

THE WOMAN WITH THE PERFUME
(Mark 14:1-9)

Have you come to see me?
        Do you know who I am?
Of course, everyone thinks they know who I am...
Or who I 'should' be:
        a proper daughter,
        a proper wife,
        a proper mother...
And everyone is quick to cluck their tongues
        when I do something 'improper' –
Like my clothes:
        plain, dark dress for a married woman
        head covered...
But I like to celebrate –
        celebrate life and colour and being alive!

So I dress up.
And they say I look like a whore,
        and so they whisper about me.

Surely you've heard them, and you know all about me;
But if you know –
Why have you come?
        to stare?
        or to share?
No matter,

you're all most welcome;
My door is always open,
> though most would rather die than come in:
> they might get infected with my love for life!

So, who DO you think I am?
'That' woman?
> The one who does the extravagant things?
> Who doesn't understand the cost of things?
But people confuse cost with price, don't they?
> and they equate price with usefulness,
And so a great pile of bread – a year's worth! –
> is measured against a tiny jar of nard...
Usefulness
Sustenance
Measured against celebration and adoration.
> pebbles or pearls, I'd say.

If I had given him a year's worth of bread,
> what would they have done with it?
Given it all to the poor, they say –
> and what would be left of my love?
I, perhaps, would be applauded for my generosity:
> the poor would have what they needed for their bellies
> but nothing more...
But would he have been anointed?
I'm not saying we mustn't do our part to help the poor,
> but there are other things to be done as well.

Perhaps it's like a plain black dress
> and a fancy, extravagant scarf –
The plain black dress to cover the essentials;
> the scarf to express the joy of living.
Bread to exist;
> beauty to express...

Can we live without beauty?
Is there life without beauty?

Is there life where there is no love?

Beauty and love:
> that's what he brought into my life.

Existing is what I was already doing:
> Going from day to day
> Doing the existence things.
> Eating and sleeping and meeting their demands.
> Finding myself eroded away bit by bit
>> by the meaninglessness of it all.

I began to believe there was nothing about me
> that was loveable.
I was just serviceable,
> something to keep others comfortable.

He didn't see me like that.
I wasn't just a body to keep him happy.
> I was the person inside –
A Child of God, he called me –
> with heart and head and hands
> that could love and live and laugh.

It was more than I could imagine:
It was the difference between a loaf of bread
> and a bottle of perfume.

Both can be shared, of course.
Bread is safe because it's cheap
> And no one takes much notice.
But when you've found what you really want,
> Do you settle for cheap?

He told us he was like bread for us –
And he was:
> Sustaining
> Nourishing

Fulfilling our needs

But he was more than that.
His love was like the smell of the perfume
      all over the house
      out the windows
      out the doors
            not to be contained
            not to be restricted
      only to flow out and over
            covering all
            filling all
            empowering all.
      Empowering us to love in return.

Once you've been loved that way –
      for who you are and all you're meant to be –
      you want to share it.

When you're loved for who you are
      you're free to love others the same way.

Not that others will understand or accept the love –
So many are blinded with concerns
      about money
      about politics
      and who will win
      and who will die
      and who will be overcome...

We will all have concerns.
We will all die.
The question is: who of us is willing to live?
      Who is willing to love?
      Who is willing to love the reality of our being?
            The preciousness of each person?

If I had a thousand bottles of nard,

I would break them all for him.
>No matter what they said.
>No matter what they did.
>No matter that they barred me from the house
>>or the town,
>or even tried to kill me.

You can't kill love.
I know they will try.
I know they will try to kill him.
They will think that is the answer to their problem.
They are wrong.

They will try to bar the door to love.
Love's door is always open.
My door will always be open.

They try to distance themselves from people like me.
Of course, they would never invite me in to be one of them.
One who doesn't understand beauty
>calls it Shame.
And one doesn't invite Shame in;
>one invites Honour.
They think I am shame
>because they don't know what love is about.
At least Simon knew he was Honour —
>perhaps because Simon was a leper.
He knew well about shame and honour.
But the others,
What did they know?
That love is more than recognition of what you've done
>or who your father is?

Jesus knows love.
He looks past our shame
>our littleness
>our disregard
>as if it were not there.

All the things that make others want to avoid us,
He accepts and transforms.
He welcomes us in,
      allows us to weep
      to laugh
      to love
      to live
      to be forgiven
      to be real.

He saw past what I was:
      tired, broken, worn –
And knew me for what I could be:
      alive, whole, energised.

And suddenly I saw him as he was:
      the wholly alive Holy One,
      whose presence radiated Life
          and Love
          and authority.

But I also saw what he could so easily be:
      fragile
      broken
      forsaken
      abandoned.

Oh! My God! No!
Love cannot be left to be trampled upon!

In that moment I knew what I had to do.
The bottle had stayed on my shelf many years
      gathering dust
      but too precious to throw out.
A 'gift' from years before –
      another love, another time, another place:
A lavish gift from one who knew nothing of
      True Worth

Or True Love.
It was a compensation, I knew,
      for guilt.

But just as Jesus had ignored
      the gaudiness of my packaging
      and seen the worth within me,
I knew he would see past the guilt offering.
As he transformed me,
      he would understand the transformation of such a gift
      from guilt
      to gratitude.

Why aren't there better words to express?
What could I say?
Nothing.

What could I do?
Only this:
Offer what I had
      to the most beautiful one I had ever encountered.

Break open the fast-closed bottle.
Allow its fragrance to fill the room
      the house
      the village.
Let its aroma shout to all who passed by:
      He's here!
      The Beloved!
      The Beautiful One!

Do what I could do:
Anoint his head
      a head which could so easily be crushed
      by those who couldn't or wouldn't see.

Do what I could do!
Wash his feet with my tears

and wipe them with my hair.

Do what I could do!

Of course they didn't understand.
They told me to use the perfume for the poor.
The poor wouldn't profit from my perfume.
It would only stay bottled up
        or cover up the stench of stolen favours.

No, the only use for this perfume
        was to adorn the only one who merited its beauty.

He seemed to understand.
Of course he would!
Beauty understands beauty.
Love acknowledges love.
        And its aroma never fully disappears.

I can smell it even now.
It lingers in the air
        like a Spirit unleashed.
The Spirit of Love unleashed,
        never to die
        never to be captured and bottled up again,
But free to inhabit
        any who dare invite it in.

He said I would be remembered for what I had done,
        but that wasn't why I did it.
It wasn't me I wanted them to remember.
It was Him.
It was Love
        not to be captured,
        only to be released.

And so, I release you, my friend.
I release you to go on your way –

not bottled or kept away safely
but to be fully unleashed to change a dreary world
into a place of beauty and love.
Amen!

THE WOMAN WITHOUT THE PERFUME
(Matthew 26:6-13)

Well, it was *embarrassing!*
      That's the only way I can think of describing it.
I mean, there she was, sailing into the dinner party –
      I don't even think anyone had even *invited* her!
I mean, I'm quite sure my master, Simon, hadn't –
Sure, he's a leper, and all,
      and so he thinks and chooses his friends
      a little differently than others.
But even HE would know
      she wasn't the type for that kind of dinner party....

In the first place, she should have known it would just be men.
She should have been able to see that the moment
      she walked in the front door!
I certainly knew it – from behind the kitchen door –
This was not a dinner party for women...
      unless she thought she was to be the entertainment! Hah!

No, it wasn't that sort of party...
It was just a quiet gathering for Simon's new friend, Jesus,
      and some of his followers.
Simon was *very* impressed with them all –
      very impressed that Jesus had taken an interest in him
When so many still rejected him –
      even after he was cured of his leprosy

and the priests had all acknowledged it –
Ah yes, things have been hard for my master –
But he has taken it well,
        and he has done his best to pull his life back together...

But then SHE comes waltzing into the house!
I suppose the way she came in,
        she really couldn't see that she was out of place.
She only had eyes for Jesus...

And who wouldn't have eyes for Jesus?
        I mean, he is one lovely specimen of manhood!
Hard to imagine why he never married –
        not like Simon with his leprosy –
        or me with my limp...
He was just – just perfection!
        and not just in body,
        but in mind and spirit –
And when he looked at you!
        Oh my!
Well, it wasn't the way other men look at you –
It was with a gentleness,
        but also a fierceness – a fierceness for truth
        and justice and ...
Well, when he looked at you,
You felt like he knew you through and through –
        but you didn't have to be embarrassed
Because whatever he saw
        he blessed,
        and you just felt blessed being in his presence.

I suppose that's what *she* felt, too –
        the peace
        the acceptance
        the joy of knowing you don't have to hide your wounds.
Oh my!
I'm starting to sound like what she did was right!
        I don't mean that at all.

I mean, you know you're safe with Jesus –
        and you want him to know that you know that –
But you DON'T go throwing yourself at him!
        Literally!
        You don't!
        Especially at a dinner party!
        Especially at someone else's house!
        Especially when you're the only woman in the room!
        Especially when you haven't been invited!

You just DON'T.
It's not proper.
Even if Jesus has different ideas about what's proper.
You just don't.

Oh, Jesus.
Oh, my Lord.
Jesus, you know I've never actually spoken to you —
I wouldn't know how to start
        or where or what to say...
But I suppose it wouldn't matter to you.

You didn't turn her away.
It must have been terribly embarrassing for you,
        especially when she was crying
        and pouring out the perfume on your head
        and the whole room was filling with the smell –
It nearly knocked me off my feet here in the kitchen!
        It blocked out the aroma of the roasting meat!
Turned everything upside down!

But you didn't turn her away.
You didn't scold her.
You scolded the ones that scolded her.

Oh, Lord! That would have been me, too!

Oh, Lord! Have I offended you
      by taking offence at her?

Oh, no! my Lord!

I can see it now.
I was just like the rest of them, wasn't I?
      and she was the only one who understood?
I, poor, miserable kitchen slave that I am –
I was using their shield of respectability
      to try to promote myself
And all I've done is further myself
      from expressing the love she knew...

Oh, Lord, what have I done?

Is there any hope for me?

If I called you back to this house again –
      in my mind, of course!
      for I could never speak to you directly –
Would you come again
      and let me just sit near?

I wouldn't do the perfume –
I *couldn't* do the perfume –
It would be all my year's wages!
It's not my style...
I'm just the galley girl –
      peeling the potatoes
      scrubbing the floors...

.... I have no perfume, Lord,
But I do have my tears.
Perhaps you would accept my tears?
In remembrance that I, too, have loved you?

MRS NICODEMUS
(John 3:1-17)

He was out again tonight –
        I always get a bit nervous when he's out after dark.
I'd like him to carry a torch with him,
        but he thinks that would attract too much attention.
Not that my Nick is a particularly private man —
He's respectable: he is a Pharisee, of course!
He doesn't go out shouting and waving his arms around,
        nor is he the kind that prays loudly in the street
                to attract attention.
But he can speak his mind when he needs to.

My Nick is a thoughtful one.
        Sometimes I tell him he's too thoughtful.
Sometimes he just will NOT let go of something
        that he's mulling over.
Sometimes he just drives me crazy with his thinking through...
I tell him: Give it a rest, Nick.
        You don't have to understand everything in the world!
        The sun will still rise tomorrow
        even if you haven't figured everything out tonight.

But it's hard for him to 'give it a rest.'
        He will mull it over, look at it this way, that way.
        upside down, inside out
        until he understands...

That's how it was when he first heard about Jesus.
      He'd come home brimming over with stories
      about the things he'd heard
      and the things he'd seen.
He wanted to tell me about that wedding at Cana
      where Jesus turned the water to wine
And then that incident in the temple
      when Jesus turned the tables into splinters
      and sent the sheep and goats on a stampede.
How Jesus had said if the whole thing was destroyed,
      he'd build it back up again — by himself!
 About how things had to change at the temple
      with our systems, our tradition –
Sounded positively dangerous to me –
      what with the Romans all about —
But to Nick it was intriguing.
      He'd come back in the evening with stories to tell
         and questions rolling out thick and fast
         and eyes eager with interest.
Hardly able to settle at night...
      His body tossing and turning on his mat,
      as his thoughts tossed and turned in his head...

So I wasn't too surprised when he went out
      that night some time back...
Some have whispered about it to me —
      that they'd seen my husband going out after dark
      and wondering where he'd been going...
Not exactly respectable behaviour for a Pharisee!

When I asked him straight out where he had been,
      he suddenly looked at me
         like he was seeing me for the first time.
It would be easy to say his eyes were wide open in panic,
      but I've known him long enough to recognise the intrigue.
He'd seen something that had grabbed his attention —
      and it wasn't letting go.

He told me he'd been to see Jesus.
He told me about their strange conversation –
>how Jesus was talking about being born again, born from above
>born in a new way...

I wondered what two men knew about childbirth!
They might have observed the months of a woman waiting
>of a belly growing bigger and harder
>>till it was ready to burst;
They might have heard the moans or even screams
>from the birthing tent;
They would have seen the newborn –
>and the exhausted mother —
But what did they know of being born or of giving birth!

Nick said Jesus spoke of being born of 'water and spirit;'
Plenty of water with a birthing!
>Water whooshing out and exploding everywhere –
>Uncontrollable!
Plenty of Spirit as well...
>Spirit-breath giving life to flesh.
The heaving gasps of the mother giving her all to the forces
>of pushing the baby from one world into the next.
That first gulping breath that the child takes in,
>suddenly finding itself in a completely new territory:
Air to breathe;
>cool breeze on its skin
>>after months in the warm and cosy womb.
Limbs to stretch in ways that increasingly weren't possible
>while still cramped inside.
Ears hearing sounds that were familiar inside
>but now came from somewhere outside.
Eyes experiencing light for the first time —
>dare one peek out at the brightness?
A throat finding a voice
>that had never been used or heard before
>calling out: I'm here!

But where am I?
>Everything has changed...

Water and Spirit,
Flesh and Blood,
Being Born, giving Birth...
>everything is new...

I watched Nicodemus carefully that night
>when he came back from seeing Jesus -
I listened to his words and studied his face
>as he described what he had heard –
His eyes had that wildness –
>almost as if he'd giving birth himself:
Jesus talking about the coming Kingdom of God
>as if it were like childbirth —
>as if coming into God's presence was like being born —
>everything is changed; everything is new.

I listened hard to Nicodemus, but I didn't need to say much.
He didn't really notice my silence,
>because he had so much to think about himself.
He started to explain that he'd asked Jesus
>how one could re-enter his mother's womb...
But he looked at me sideways as he told me,
>and I could see he knew
>>that Jesus meant something different.
I knew he wasn't taking Jesus' words literally –
>and that he knew Jesus wasn't speaking literally either.
Jesus was trying to described something indescribable:
>and the best language he could use
>was about the journey from womb to waking world...

That gave me plenty to think about that night.
>Nicodemus had plenty to think about as well —
Both of us feeling as though we were standing
>on the edge of a vast adventure
And adventure was calling us, daring us

to take that first step.

As we lay there deep into the night,
        Nicodemus reached over to give my hand a squeeze.
He whispered that Jesus had also said that making the journey
        involved trusting in him;
'Believing' was the word he used...
        believing that we too could be part of the world Jeus knew;
That being part of that world
        wasn't just about following all the rules —
        we'd done that all our lives!
It was about trusting and believing
        in a love that went beyond the rules...

He was silent for while
        and I thought he'd finally gone to sleep.
But then he whispered that
        the rules had been there to teach us about love...
I reached over and gave him a soft kiss—
        and we both were soon asleep.

That night was some time ago now.
In the days that followed,
        we both had listened and watched intently
        to see and hear what Jesus would be doing next.
There were more stories on the grapevine
        about Jesus' encounters with other folk:
        Jews AND Gentiles, crowds and individuals
People you'd think a Jewish teacher
        would never get involved with:
        a Samaritan woman!
        common folk gathering at the seaside...
Many of the stories seemed to have something to do with water:
        not just the water and the wine at the wedding.
        but the 'living water' with the woman at the well
        or Jesus walking on the water
        or Jesus talking about 'rivers of living water'
                flowing at the Festival.

I kept thinking about the waters of childbirth...

After Jesus healed a blind man,
       he talked with the Pharisees
              about seeing for the first time,
       which made me think about a newborn baby
              first opening its eyes...
The stories circulated about the blind man seeing and believing,
       and that reminded me
       of that middle-of-the night conversation with my Nick
       and what Jesus meant by 'believing.'

Not everyone seemed to grasp what Jesus was talking about,
       especially some of the other Pharisees
       who seemed especially threatened by Jesus' words...
I often wondered what they were afraid of!
       Does a baby fear its birth?
       Does a baby have to 'believe' to be born?

It was an evening not long after that my Nick came home
       with his brow knitted up in thought once again...
The temple police were in debate with the other Pharisees—
       apparently some of the police — and the crowds
       saw something in Jesus,
Something special that made them wonder
       why so many of the Pharisees were hell-bent
              on dismissing and destroying Jesus.
Nicodemus was troubled.
After a long, tense hour of quiet turmoil,
       he blurted out that he had spoken publicly
              to his fellow religious leaders.
He had reminded them that the Law requires
       that an accused be given a trial –
Even as he told me what he'd said,
       he admitted that he'd probably stretched the Law a bit,
But even if it didn't say exactly that — that was its intent:
       that it was important to listen carefully to what people said –
       to hear what they really meant.

And just because what one heard might not agree
       with what one thought one *knew*
       that didn't mean it wasn't true.

Again, it was a restless night for my Nick — and for me.
And the days and nights that followed weren't much better.
The storm clouds grew in the public debates
       even while Jesus showed more and more signs
       and tried to explain through more and more words:
              how the world God wanted for us all
              was constructed not of condemning laws
              but of loving justice.
Those were difficult words to understand
       and difficult signs to make sense of
              when one was accustomed to everyday life.

I kept pondering those words
       about birth and water and spirit and new life...
Especially as I heard about Jesus washing his disciples' feet
       and the feast before the Passover.
Who washes one's servants' feet?!?

There was the 'water' again –
       but the way it was being used was all topsy-turvy –
       against all the rules and customs
       unless the Law WAS about loving...

But in a strange and calming way,
       it began to make perfect sense,
Even if I couldn't really describe it rationally to anyone else.
       Nick couldn't either. But we both kept trying.

You will have heard by now what happened after that...
How the authorities finally decided
       to take matters into their own hands.
About how they had the mock trial
       and how they flogged him
       and how... how they crucified him...

And how, even when he was hanging there on the cross,
      they stabbed a spear through his side —
      right where his womb would have been
          if he were a woman —

And the water and the blood – and the Spirit – poured out.
Just like he was giving birth.

Except he had died.

My Nick came back very late that night.
He'd rushed back in several times that afternoon and evening —
Our eyes had met once or twice.
      His eyes were focussed and determined.
      His mouth firm and set.
It was the Sabbath, and he should have been resting.
      I lit the candles; I said the prayers on my own.
He was assembling a huge stash of myrrh and aloes
      weighing nearly as much as himself!
He only spoke briefly to say that he and his friend Joseph
      were paying a burial fit for a King.
The sabbath Law was being exchanged for a labour of Love.

When he returned, late, late in the night,
      He went silently to the sleeping mat....
After a while, I could hear his silent sobs.
      As I reached over, I could feel the tears on his cheek.
Sobs of Spirit;
      Waters of Cleansing?
      Promises of new birth seemingly dissolving into...what?
==
It is the morning of the sabbath now.
The sun is hiding behind the clouds;
      everywhere is silent and in darkness.
I have been trying to tell you this story,
      though in reality, there are no words to tell it properly.
The words seem to be holding their breath
      as if the Spirit is waiting, waiting...

No one would believe me if I said it out loud —
      but it feels very much
Like waiting for New Birth...
We wait....

MARY MAGDALENE
(John 20:1-18)

When you are one of the people in the shadows,
    whom others ignore or take for granted,
There is a certain freedom
    in being able to slip in and out of situations unnoticed.
People don't expect anything from you,
    so you're free to do things
    which respectable people might not imagine or dare.

On that Sunday morning,
    when everything had gone so terribly wrong,
    there was nothing to keep me in my bed
        after the Sabbath restrictions were finished.
It was dark that morning
    and I hadn't slept, for days it seemed
Who can sleep when your world has fallen apart?
    Who can sleep when evil is all around?
    Who can sleep when every rustle
        speaks of imminent danger?
    Who can sleep when fear grips every fibre of your being?
    When you cannot close your eyes
        for the horror that is inside your head?
    When the convulsions of grief that rack your body
        have finally paralyzed all you knew or wanted
            or cared about?
Who can sleep

when all you have hoped and dreamed of
Has been destroyed,
> demolished,
> beaten,
> broken,
> tortured,
> tormented,
> crushed,
> crucified?

I couldn't sleep –
Not for those two eternal nights
> when the world stopped its breathing
> while the men kept murmuring their Sabbath prayers
> and the women fumbled through the motions
> > of lighting the candles and serving the food.
They sent me out
> for I kept dropping everything
And I certainly couldn't eat.
Who can eat
> when every dish carries visions of crucified flesh?
Who can eat when one's throat is gagged
> as if by a giant tombstone?

Before the stars melted away that dark morning,
> I left my tormented pillow,
> gathered the spices,
> and went to the tomb in the garden unnoticed,
Just to be near the place
> where his body lay.
Perhaps his Spirit might still linger.
> Just to be near again.

I could still hear his voice in my ears,
> even though his gruesome crucifixion
> had taken away the flimsy hope
> that somehow things would eventually be different...
His mission had failed,

which in some ways put us to where we'd been before:
    a people resigned to being victim of imperial abuse...
And yet, we'd caught a glimpse of what-could-be,
    A people building a new society,
    one built on peace and joy and the love of God.
It had all seemed so real, so possible, while he walked with us...

I could still hear his voice in my ears...
    'This is the way; I am the way.'

So I crept out that morning, while it was still dark...
    to see, to be,
    to be close again.

But what I saw when I was close was all so confusing:
    The stone rolled back, the grave empty,
    no body lying there in its mangled grief...
Only a stillness...

I went and told the men –
    and they hurried to see as well...
But then they went back home again...
    confused, afraid.
I wasn't ready to go home.
    What was there at home now?

I peered into the grave again –
    deep into its emptiness —
But from the emptiness shone back a bright stillness.
Through my tears, I realised there were figures there as well –
    could they be angels?

I held my breath, trying not to weep too loudly,
    biting my lip, trying to think...
And then they spoke —
    I hadn't heard an angel speak before –
They asked me why I was crying.
    Why *wouldn't* I be crying?

My best friend and the hope of the world
    had been killed!

I sensed another presence and turned around –
    Still another angel?
    Was I being surrounded?
But this presence spoke my name...
    and when he spoke, I knew that voice –
It was my Master!
    How could it be?
    He was dead.
    He was finished.
    He was gone!
No! It couldn't be!
But ... Yes! It was!
    It was my Lord!
    It was my Teacher!
    It was my Love!
    It was my Life!

I wanted to dance
    to laugh and cry
    and sing and shout.
I wanted to hold him tight
    and never let him go again.

But he kept me at a distance,
    saying something strange
        about not yet being ascended...
    I didn't know what all that meant,
Only that he was still with me,
    yet it was different...

In a moment's flash I realised
    that all we had had together
Was what we still had now:
    spirit, hope, peace, joy...
And that he was still with me,

but from here on it would be different...

The Spirit I had always felt from him was still there,
       but it was more powerful now.
I recognised I needed to keep some distance,
       and yet that distance did not disturb the presence.
We were still together,
       we were still one with each other in the Spirit.
       I was still energised and empowered,
       but it was different now.

He told me to go and tell the brothers again –
I thought of those whom I had told just a short while before –
How they had come and looked for themselves
       but run back home again.

But now I had seen – and heard –
       and was starting to understand...
       that everything we'd hoped and dreamed of,
       everything we'd experienced of how the world might be,
           the love and joy and peace we'd experienced,
       was not destroyed, only being transformed...

And somehow, folks like me,
       who had previously lived in the shadows,
       were coming into a new and brilliant light.
We had no idea where that light might shine
       or what it might illumine in the future,
But it was ours to share:
       tell the brothers,
       tell the sisters,
       tell the houses and the trees and the flowers and birds!
We who had been silent were to shout to the sky
       and sing to the heavens:
       "He is alive!
       I have seen the Lord!"
And nothing, nothing will ever be the same!
       Amen!

TABITHA-DORCAS
(Acts 9:36-43)

Have you met Tabitha-Dorcas?
> She's my neighbour and my friend!
Some people call her by her Aramaic name: Tabitha.
The Greeks call her Dorcas.
I call her Tabitha-Dorcas
> because one name alone isn't big enough
> to tell you all about her.
Whether Tabitha or Dorcas,
> she was loved by all!
And why not?
> She was good to everybody,
> especially those of us who were widows
> > and didn't have much.
But she was good to other people, too –
She loved everybody,
> and that's why everybody loved her.

Some people say she's why Joppa is such a nice place to live.
Sure, we're blessed to be on the seaside,
> so we have plenty of fish,
And we have our own famous orange groves
> and all the business that comes with fruit and fish
> and everything else that Palestine needs or sells...
You might have heard the old story of Jonah,

so you'll know that Joppa was where he headed
when he wanted to *get* somewhere!

Yes, Joppa is a busy place,
          an important place,
          with lots of different things going on
          and lots of different people interacting.
Sometimes that's a blessing
          and sometimes it's a curse:
It's a curse when people can't get on together,
          when they think that
                    just because the others speak a little differently
          or grew up somewhere else
          or trade in a different kind of goods —
Some people think that
          just because we're not all doing the same things
          or talking the same language,
                    that somehow we're different inside.
Then there's all kinds of trouble:
          people mistrusting each other
          and shutting their doors and windows tight at night
          and pretending they don't hear when trouble calls out.
It's times like that
          when living together with different kinds of people
                    can be a curse.

But when Tabitha-Dorcas is with us, it's not like that.
Everyone knows that whoever they are
          she'll take them in and help any way she can!
Palestinians, Jews, Greek, we're all just people to her,
          and she calls each of us her best friend.

You'll know that Tabitha-Dorcas
          has always been good with sewing
          and making things with her hands.
She could have sold her things for piles and piles of money,
But she didn't: she gave it all away,
          gave it away to whoever needed it,

148

but mostly to whoever needed it most.
She wouldn't let you pay her:
  she'd say that God had given her all she needed,
That she'd been blessed,
  and it was her job to share the blessings with others.
And if we wanted to say, 'Thank you,'
  we should just go ahead and share with others, too,
So the blessings would just keep multiplying.

And when you stop to think about it,
  that's exactly what happened to us here in Joppa.
Tabitha-Dorcas showed us how to bless each other,
  and we just got so busy blessing
  that we didn't have time to stir up fights,
  even with the ones who were a bit different.

It wasn't only her sewing and her money that she shared.
She shared her prayers and her religion with us too.
There were lots of religions going around in Joppa,
  but Tabitha-Dorcas told everyone she met
  that she was a disciple of the holy man, Jesus,
  the one who came from Galilee.
He never actually got here to Joppa,
  but some of his followers did,
And they told Tabitha-Dorcas,
  and she told the rest of us.

She told us – and she showed us –
That this Jesus had blessed people, all kinds of people,
  and that he made sure that even the poorest people
   got what they needed:
  that he provided food and drink
   when they were hungry and thirsty
  and he actually healed those who were sick
  and he talked to children and women
   and slaves and tax collectors –
The way Tabitha-Dorcas told it, he loved everybody!
So she got pretty fed up with religious people

who only wanted to help people
　　　who looked like themselves
　　　and already lived in comfortable houses.
No, she told us that Jesus said God loves everybody,
　　　and if that was what God was doing,
　　　shouldn't she – and we — be doing it, too?

Tabitha-Dorcas said that a lot of religious and powerful people
　　　had got upset that Jesus was helping people
　　　　　who didn't deserve help.
She said they got the political authorities going against him
　　　and they actually crucified him!
Tabitha-Dorcas always drew her breath in sharply
　　　when she got to that part of the story.
And then she would be quiet for a while,
　　　and her needle would stop mid-stitch,
And you could see how much it hurt her
　　　to think of people killing –
　　　　　actually murdering! – anyone,
　　　but especially someone who had so much love to share.

But then a huge smile would burst out on Tabitha-Dorcas' face,
　　　like a big sunrise –
And she would tell us with a hearty laugh
　　　that THAT wasn't the end of it!
God had had the last laugh,
And Jesus had been raised up – from the dead!
　　　and didn't that just PROVE –
　　　couldn't everybody see from that —
　　　　　that God was saying Jesus was absolutely right!
We're all supposed to be helping each other!
　　　Loving each other!
　　　Doing everything we possibly can to bless each other!

And the people who were running around scared –
　　　scared of each other, scared of death, scared of the law,
　　　scared of the religious authorities –
Well, they just didn't know.

You don't have to be afraid of ANYTHING
        if you were doing what was good and right and true;
If you were following Jesus' ways
        and had Jesus' spirit with you,
God's goodness would prevail in the end.

By that time, Tabitha-Dorcas would be mostly finished
        with whatever it was she was making,
And you soon found yourself going home
        with a new apron or a new scarf
        or something for the grandbaby
        or a warmer blanket for the bed...
And a warmer place in your heart
        for all the love she'd shared.

Sometimes when new people came into Joppa,
They would be a little suspicious of Tabitha-Dorcas:
        why would anyone want to be giving everything away?
        And what of a *woman*
                who calls herself a 'disciple' of a holy man?
        Wasn't that something only a man could do?
        Be a disciple?
Well, Tabitha-Dorcas didn't think so.
She said Jesus was for everybody,
        and anybody could follow him.
So it wasn't long before the newcomers
        would be invited in as well,
        and they would stop to hear her stories,
And before they knew it, they'd be smiling and laughing
        and sharing stories with her.
        and soon they would be taking home
                a new cloth for their widowed mothers –
        and telling everyone Tabitha-Dorcas
                was their new best friend...

That's how it was for us in Joppa.
That's how it IS for us in Joppa.
We know we were blessed

because Tabitha-Dorcas loved each of us
and told us God loved us, too, just as Jesus said.

And then came the day we'd all dreaded:
the day that Tabitha-Dorcas died.
We couldn't quite believe it in the beginning.
but when we went to see,
there was her body, cold and still.
At first it was hard to recognise her
because her hands and her mouth were still as well!

We stood staring for a while,
trying to remember what to do
without Tabitha-Dorcas there to tell us how to help...

Then someone remembered Tabitha-Dorcas
telling us about Peter –
one of Jesus' closest disciples who lived in our area –
just a half-day's journey away in Lydda.
She'd told us that Peter was the one who Jesus had told
to take care of things after he was gone

He'd told him to take care of his mother –
even while he was dying on the cross.
And afterwards, he'd told him to 'feed his lambs'
and 'take care of his sheep.'
Some of our men set out to find this Peter
and ask him to give a final blessing
for our Tabitha-Dorcas.

Those of us who were left behind
ran to our houses
and brought back the garments she'd given us.
And we cleaned and anointed
and wrapped her body in the clothes
so we could give her the decent burial she deserved.

We were just finishing when the men arrived with Peter.

He was bigger than I'm imagined.
You could tell he was a fisherman:
      strong and rugged from the wind and salt.
He was brash, too.
I wondered if he had been offended when Jesus told him
      to take care of lambs.
The fishermen I know certainly don't know much about lambs!
And he was so big and bold
      that for a moment I thought he'd be angry with us
      for calling him away to take care of a dead widow.
I started to open my mouth to tell him
      what a great lady she was –
      the Founder of the Joppa Women's Working Party! –
The one who had taught us all how to help and bless each other,
      how to love each other –
But before I could say a word,
      he was ushering all of us widows out of the room
          and closing the door.

We all stood quietly outside to listen,
      our hearts pounding loudly!
We could hear his voice,
      but it wasn't at all loud or boisterous.
      It was bold, but it was gentle, too.
We looked at each other and realised
      that he was praying for Tabitha-Dorcas
      just the way she had prayed for each of us.
He was asking for God's Kingdom to come to us –
      here in Joppa –
          just as Tabitha-Dorcas had done so many times.
He was asking that our sins be forgiven –
      and that we would have
          the bread we needed for the day.
We thought of the bread and the wine
      and the clothing she had given us
And our eyes filled with tears.

And then we heard him say, 'Tabitha, get up.'

We peered inside –
    and there was Tabitha-Dorcas
        sitting up and smiling at everyone again!

Oh, my goodness!
Can you imagine the shrieking and laughing
    and crying and carrying on that followed!
We were all hugging each other
    the men and women alike –
I even gave Big Brash Peter a squeeze!
    He looked a little surprised —
        I guess they don't do that sort of thing much in Galilee.

But this is Joppa.
    And there's a lot of joy in Joppa.
Enough, in fact, to convince Peter to stay a while longer.

He moved in with Simon the Tanner for a while.
I think he would have liked to do a bit of fishing,
    but we insisted he spend most of his time
    telling us the rest of the stories about Jesus,
    the ones Tabitha-Dorcas hadn't heard yet.
It was like having a festival every day to hear his stories!

Tabitha-Dorcas showed him all around the city,
    and when they came to any of our houses,
    we would show him all the clothes
        and all things she had made for us.
At first he seemed a little surprised that she took him
    to so many different houses – Greek and Jew...
He wasn't quite sure how to act –
    a little like a fish out of water, you might say,
But in time, he warmed to the Joppa spirit.

A week or so later, it seemed a man named Cornelius in Lydda
    had a vision in which he was sent to see Peter in Joppa,
Something about which food he was allowed to eat.
We knew that when Peter had first come

he would only eat kosher,
and we did our best to get him what he needed,

But this Cornelius arrived telling about a dream
that said it was OK to eat any food...
And he said he'd been sent to Peter, right here in Joppa
with Simon the Tanner...

In the end, it seems Peter was convinced by Cornelius' dream.
He was less nervous after that,
less anxious about going into Greek houses,
about talking to widows,
about just accepting people as they were,
about having a blessing ready for everyone.

Some other newcomers have arrived in Joppa.
They knew Peter from before,
and they say he's changed as well...
I joined in the conversation – it's a way we Joppa folk have –
and I told them I'd met Mr Cornelius
and Mr Peter too,
and they were both good and blessed men.

But I wondered if they'd met my friend, Tabitha-Dorcas?
because she was the one who'd taught us all
about being blessed
and using our blessings to bless others,
No matter who the other was
or where they'd come from.
And she was the one who'd first told us about Jesus.
Had they met Jesus, too?
If they hadn't, I'd take them to Tabitha-Dorcas
and she'd tell them all about him –
And if they had time to sit and chat for a while,
she'd probably make something for them as well!
And the blessings would just keep flowing.

APPHIA
(Philemon)

Well, the invitation has arrived,
      and we're all planning to go!
It hardly seems possible that our own Onesimus –
      once our slave –
      is now to be our bishop!
Paul would have been so proud!
Philemon would have been proud!
Both of them have gone on now –
      joined the heavenly band
            of brothers and sisters of the King!
But we who are still here with the earthly band,
      we're proud as we can be today
That the world has finally seen our Onesimus for who he is –
      the 'Useful One,' just as his name implies...

The 'Useful One' ....
Paul was the first to really claim him as such.
At the time, we were all thinking of him as rather 'Useless' –
      and Paul called us on that one!
I think it came out first in his letter –
      the short one he wrote directly to us from the prison.
Paul, of course, was always writing letters,
      mostly long epistles that took the whole of Sunday
      to be read aloud at our gathering –
      and then we would keep them for a while

and discuss them
and read them again
and discuss some more
and finally pass them on to another gathering...
There was always so much to digest in those letters,
and while we were reluctant to pass them on,
We always knew another would soon be making its way to us,
having been well-digested and discussed
by another congregation...

Some thought our letter,
the one addressed to Philemon as the head of the household
and to me and to Archippus and our house church,
Some thought it not so important because it was so short
and perhaps too 'business-like' instead of 'spiritual' ...
But what a wealth of love it contained!
Not so much of Paul's theologizing and sermonizing,
But Paul at his best –
addressing a very practical problem
with a spiritual wisdom and foresight
far beyond our own...

There were some who took great exception to the letter!
Oh! There were some disagreements there!
It wasn't so terribly unusual to receive such a letter,
A letter begging for merciful treatment of a returned slave,
especially when the slave accompanied the letter!
But this letter was so different.
It spoke of Onesimus as a 'brother,'
a much beloved one at that!
And it was very difficult for a lot of people
to wrap their minds around that concept –
That a slave could become a 'brother,'
that is – 'one of us' – 'in the flesh' was how Paul put it.
Part of the family, so to speak.

I remember Onesimus when he arrived with that letter
standing there in the doorway and trembling visibly,

head bowed and knuckles gripped tightly behind his back
    as he handed over the letter and awaited his verdict.
Would he be whipped? Beaten?
    Starved?
    Executed?

And then there was Philemon's hearty laugh –
    Onesimus' head jerked up to see if it were kind or cruel…
But who could ever think Philemon cruel?
    aristocratic, perhaps –
    maybe even a bit arrogant at times…
But since he had heard Paul's preaching about the Christ,
    he had become a different man.
He laughed and brushed away the quick tear
    and shook his head and said to himself as much as anyone,
    'Oh, Paul! You always know how to turn the situation on its head!'

Then it was just like the stories we'd heard that Jesus had told,
    Like the one about the renegade son who had come back home:
Philemon was welcoming Onesimus back as his own brother
    instead of his renegade slave,
    giving him the best seat,
    bringing him food and drink,
    and wanting to hear all about
        how Paul was faring these days in prison…

Some of the others weren't so happy to see all that.
    Many thought Onesimus should at least be whipped.
After all, what would the other slaves think?
    Soon they'd all be running after Paul as well!
Still others listened as the letter was read out
    and thought that Paul
        was really just trying to get Onesimus
            as his own slave…
    seeing Philemon as a soft touch…
Others laughed behind his back
    and whispered to each other their doubts
    about just what kind of 'repayment'

Paul would be able to offer
for the debts Onesimus had incurred...
How would an old man in prison be able to repay debts?

They were the ones who really didn't understand
    what it was all about.
They were the ones who said, 'My brother, my sister'
    with their mouths,
But with their actions,
        they treated each other with worldly patterns –
        sneering and excluding the ones
            they considered beneath them,
        bowing and kowtowing to their superiors.
They never really seemed to understand that it was all different
    when we became a part of Christ's family...
As Paul put it in his letter to the folks in Galatia,
        'No longer Jew nor Greek, slave or free,
            male or female...'

In the next few days, there was no question in my mind
        that Onesimus had come back a changed man.
As Paul had pointed out, when he had been with us before,
        he was 'useless' –
        'Achrestos' was the word Paul used in his letter –
But when he came back, he was 'Euchrestos' –
        'Useful!' – just as his name implied...

It didn't take too much imagination to realise
        that Paul was using those names for Onesimus
To also point out the change that comes
        when one is united with Christ...
A-chrestos – useless *without* Christ
Eu-chrestos – of Good Use *with* Christ!

That's what it was really all about:
        The change that comes over us
        when we are united with the Christ
        and transformed by his love!

It was amazing to see it in Onesimus,
        and it reminded us to look at each other differently as well:
How each of us were bit by bit
        some slowly, some suddenly,
                becoming New Creatures in Christ's love.

Sometimes it takes the shock of having a slave returned home
        to see what a change the Christ's love makes.

Certainly Philemon saw it that day.
        even as he sat back in his chair for the evening prayers,
He couldn't keep his eyes off Onesimus –
        before, that would have been to ensure
                the Useless One didn't run off
                or steal the family jewels!
But now, it was with the pure love of a brother
        or a father –
It was as if he just couldn't contain the joy he felt
        at seeing this Useless One returned as a Brother,
        and a most Useful One at that.

Onesimus stayed with us for a while after that.
Shared with us the news of Paul and those with him in prison.
Told us, in his own halting way, his own story of running away
        and finding his true self in the preaching of Paul…
As he told the story time and again,
        we began to notice another change in him:
How his speech became more fluent,
        more assertive,
        more certain,
        even while it became more loving.

I think that was what eventually convinced Philemon
That indeed, the right thing to do,
        was to release this former slave
        into the keeping of Paul.
As I said before, many hinted broadly
        that Paul just wanted his own slave!

But it didn't really seem like that.
We could see more and more clearly
      that there was a real talent inside Onesimus –
      a real 'usefulness,' as Paul had put it –
That Onesimus was refining his profession of slavery
      into a profession of real service –
      a giving from the heart that put us all to shame!

It was that 'heart' that Paul had also spoken about –
      how Onesimus had become his own, Paul's, 'heart' as well.
And that heart of service
      Was also developing him into a man of leadership!
The sly underhanded-ness from before
      was betraying a genuine understanding
      of what needed to be done
      and how it might best be accomplished.
Where before Onesimus had gathered
      all the 'wrong' sorts of people around him,
Now he was becoming the one
      who changed those sinful hearts
      into the 'right,' into 'usefulness,'
      into brothers and sisters of love!

It was all quite amazing see...
      and we were all sad when the day came
      that Philemon sent Onesimus back to Paul.
Scarcely a dry eye in the house!
But we knew it was the best contribution we could make
      to the Kingdom work Paul was leading from the prison.

Paul didn't last much longer in the prison...
      after the Romans did away with him,
      Onesimus found other ways to make himself useful –
Soon he was back in Ephesus,
      nut no longer slothful slave –
Just as Paul had seen, he was a real leader!
He worked his way around the house groups,
      bringing the news, encouraging the disheartened,

showing the way of leadership through service and love...

And now they're to make him a bishop.
        Can you imagine?
And we're all going to go,
        even though there will probably be Roman spies all around...
        and trouble around each corner.
We MUST go!
        We must see our dear Onesimus again!
        We must celebrate that this our dear brother
                has cast off the chains of slavery
                and become a leader of freedom in Christ.
Hallelujah! Come, Lord Jesus!
Amen!

ABOUT THE AUTHOR

Bonni-Belle Pickard is a Superintendent Minister serving in the British Methodist Church. She grew up in Florida and spent twenty years teaching music at an international school in South India. She and her husband, Alfred, raised six children and currently have thirteen grandchildren. Bonni-Belle has an MDiv from Candler School of Theology in Atlanta, GA and a DMin from Wesley Theological Seminary in Washington, DC. Her previous books were *Extra Special Chocolate: Loving and Learning through International Adoption* (2019) and *Interfaith Marriage: Working for World Peace at the Most Intimate Level* (2022).

Made in the USA
Columbia, SC
28 December 2024

50756369R00096